Economy of Design of Bituminous and Concrete Pavements

A Design cum Reference Book

S.N. Sachdeva

DEDICATION

To my beloved daughter Saumya
and
my respected father Sh. Chaman Lal Sachdeva
for inspiring me
from their Heavenly Abode

CONTENTS

ACKNOWLEDGMENTS

My acknowledgements to:

Er. **C. Shanthakumar Naik**, formerly M. Tech research scholar, N.I.T. Kurukshetra, Haryana, India for help in bringing the subject matter of the book to the level of publishing.

My children Harshit and Hardik, my wife Dr. Mamta for their warmth and care, my mother Mrs Kailsh Vanti for her blessings, my family and friends for their support .

The almighty God for enabling me in all respects.

1 INTRODUCTION

1.1 GENERAL

Transportation contributes to the economic, industrial, social and cultural development of any country. Transportation is vital for the economic development of any region since every commodity produced whether it is food, clothing, industrial products or medicine needs transport at all stages from production to distribution. It provides movement of passengers and goods from one place to another place. Main modes of transportation in any country are Roadways, Railways, Waterways, and Airways. In India out of these modes, roads cater to the transportation of about 85% of passengers and 70% of goods because they are easy to construct and maintain, usually less costly, nearest to the people and also provide flexibility to movement of all kind of vehicles.

A pavement is the paved portion of a road which is used for movement of vehicles and other road users. Pavements are generally classified into two categories based on the structural behavior:

- Flexible Pavements or Bituminous Pavements
- Rigid Pavements or Cement Concrete Pavements

Flexible Pavements: Flexible pavement are those, which on the whole have low or negligible flexural strength and are rather flexible in their structural actions under the loads. The flexible pavement layers reflect the deformation of the lower layers on-to the surface of the layer. Thus if the lower layer of the pavement or soil subgrade is undulated, the flexible pavement surface also gets undulated. Bituminous concrete is one of the best flexible pavement layer materials. A typical section of a flexible pavement as shown in Figure 1.1 consists of three to four components:

- Surfacing (Wearing Course + Binder Course, for higher traffic)
- Base Course
- Sub-base Course
- Soil Subgrade

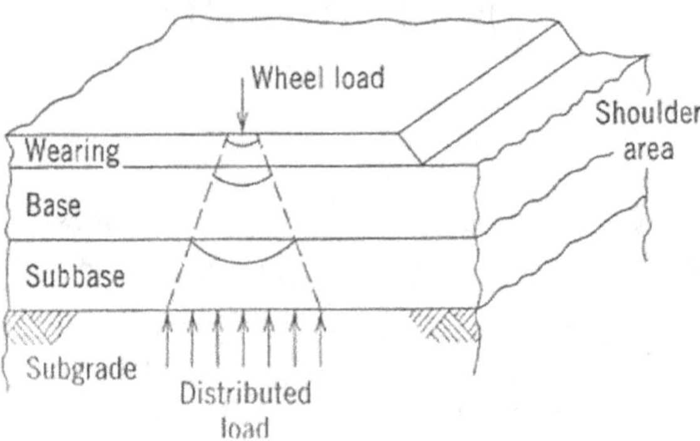

Fig.1.1 Section of a Flexible Pavement

The flexible pavement layers transmit the vertical or compressive stresses to the lower layers by grain to grain transfer through the points of contact in the granular structure. The vertical compressive stress is maximum on the pavement surface directly under the wheel load and is equal to the contact pressure under the wheel. Due to the ability to distribute the stresses to a larger area in the shape of truncated cone, the stresses get decreased at the lower layers. Therefore, by taking the advantage of the stress distribution characteristics of the flexible pavement, the layer system concept was developed. According to this, the flexible pavement may be constructed in a number of layers and the top layer has to be the strongest as the highest compressive stress are to be sustained by this layer, in addition to the wear and tear due to the traffic. The lower layers have to take up only lesser magnitudes of stresses and there is no direct wearing action due to the traffic loads, therefore inferior materials with lower cost can be used in the lower layers. The service life of a flexible pavement is typically designed in the range of 15 to 20 years.

Rigid Pavement: Rigid pavements, as the name implies, are associated with rigidity preventing them to bend under loads unlike their flexible counterparts. The rigid pavements are made of Portland Cement Concrete. The plain cement concrete slabs are expected to take up about 45 kg/cm^2 flexural stress. In case of rigid pavements, stresses are not transferred from grain to grain to the lower layers as in the case of flexible pavements. The rigid pavement has the slab action and is capable of transmitting the wheel load stresses through a wider area below. H.M Westergaard is considered the pioneer in providing the rational treatment of the rigid pavement analysis and his theory is used as the base for design of rigid pavements by IRC. The typical designed service life of a rigid pavement is between 30 and 40 years, lasting about twice as long as a flexible pavement. One major design consideration of rigid pavements is reducing fatigue failure due to the repeated stresses of traffic. Fatigue failure is common among major roads because a typical highway will experience millions of wheel passes throughout its service life. The Components of rigid pavement or cement concrete pavement structure (from top to bottom) as shown in Figure 1.2 consists of:

- Pavement Quality Concrete Slab (PQC)
- Base or Sub-base course usually of Dry Lean Concrete (DLC)
- Granular Sub-base, if needed (GSB)
- Compacted Soil Sub-grade

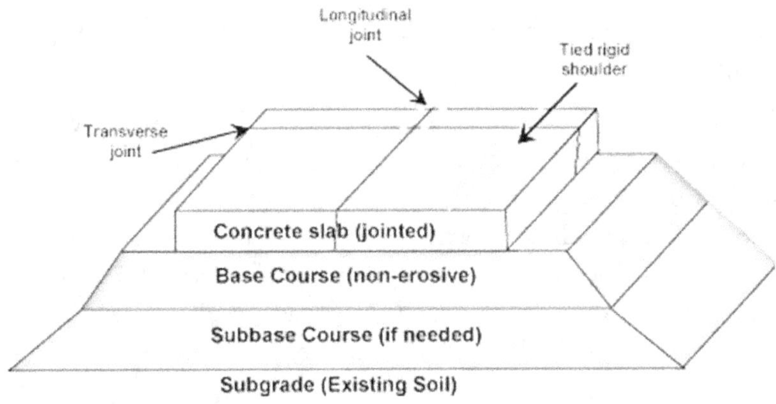

Fig.1.2 Section of a Rigid Pavement

A thin separation membrane is placed on top of the base course (dry lean concrete) before laying the PQC slab. The CC pavement is provided with the traverse and longitudinal joints. Three main types of concrete pavements commonly used are jointed plain concrete pavement (JPCP), jointed reinforced concrete pavement (JRCP) and continuously reinforced concrete pavements (CRCP).

1.2 IMPORTANCE OF ECONOMY OF DESIGN

The book "Economy of Design of Bituminous and Concrete Pavements" deals with designing the thickness of Flexible and Rigid

Pavements using latest Indian Roads Congress (IRC) recommendations given in IRC:37-2012 and IRC:58-2015 respectively and analyzing the cost of the designed pavement section with the help of Standard Data Book of Ministry of Roads Transport and Highways (MoRTH, 2003) and studying the effect of varying CBR and traffic on their thickness and cost of the pavements.

In the past, the design of Flexible pavements was based on prior experience and design was based on empirical methods. Gradually from empirical method of design, the procedure was shifted to a more mechanistic method of design. The latest design method of IRC:37-2012 is based on Mechanistic Empirical approach of design. Stronger the subgrade that is higher the California Bearing Ratio (CBR) value, the lesser thickness will be required to construct the road pavement which will result in lesser construction cost of the pavement. A lesser value of CBR indicates that a thicker pavement needs to be built to distribute the load from the wheels to the subgrade over a wider area.

Guidelines for the design of the Rigid Pavements for highways were first published in 1974. Since then a number of revisions to make the code more accurate according to the modern advancements were taken into account which included the raising of maximum axle load of commercial vehicles from 8160 kg to 10200 kg and use of computer programme IITRIGID for the computation of flexural stress due to single and tandem axle loads. The latest guidelines for the design of rigid pavements are covered in IRC:58-2015.

This book is an attempt towards designing of Flexible and Rigid pavement with varying values of CBR and traffic and studying the effect on the thickness and cost of the pavement. The importance of economy of design is that it helps in taking appropriate decision while deciding the type of pavement whether to provide a flexible pavement or a rigid pavement by knowing their initial cost of construction for given values of subgrade strength and design traffic.

The main aspects of the topic covered in the book are:
- Design of a Flexible and Rigid Pavement for varying values of subgrade strength and design traffic.
- The effect of variation in subgrade strength on thickness of the

pavement.

- The effect of variation in design traffic on thickness of the pavement.
- Cost estimation of the designed sections of the Flexible and Rigid Pavements.
- The effect of variation in Subgrade Strength on cost of the Pavement.
- The effect of variation in traffic on cost of the Pavement.
- Economy of design of flexible and rigid pavements from the point of view of their construction cost..

1.4 SCOPE

The designs undertaken in the book are valid for given values of effective CBR of soil varying from 4% to 10%, traffic 2 msa to150 msa and width of carriage way 7.5 m assumed to be located in Kurukshetra, Haryana. The designs for Flexible and Rigid Pavements have been done as per latest guidelines of IRC contained in IRC:37-2012 and IRC:58-2015 respectively. The rates of labor and materials are as per Haryana State Government approved rates whereas rate of machinery is based upon MoRTH (2003) data book. The rate analyses of various items of design have been done as per Standard Data Book of MoRTH (2003).

The philosophy covered in the book, however, can be applied to the design and cost estimation of any other road having similar roadway, traffic and soil conditions.

S.N. Sachdeva

2 IRC METHODS OF DESIGN

2.1 GENERAL

Several guidelines are available for the design of pavements for flexible and rigid pavements. Indian Roads Congress has provided the latest guidelines for the design of flexible pavements in its standard IRC:37-2012 which is based upon Mechanistic Empirical approach of design. Similarly the latest guidelines for the design of rigid pavements are covered in IRC:58-2015 which takes into account the bottom up cracking (BUC) and top down cracking (TDC) fatigue analysis. The following sections cover the relevant design guidelines of IRC.

2.2 IRC METHOD FOR DESIGN OF FLEXIBLE PAVEMENTS

The guidelines for design of flexible pavement were first brought out in1970, which were based on California Bearing Ratio (CBR) of Subgrade and traffic in terms of number of commercial vehicles (more than 3 tones laden weight) per day.

These guidelines were revised in 1984 in which design traffic was considered in terms of cumulative number of equivalent standard axle load of 80 kN in millions of standard axles (msa) and design charts were provided for traffic up to 30 msa using an empirical approach.

These guidelines were revised again in 2001 when pavements were required to be designed for traffic as high as 150 msa. The revised guidelines used a semi-mechanistic approach and the software, FPAVE was developed for the analysis and design of flexible pavements. Multilayer elastic layer theory was adopted for stress analysis of the layered elastic system.

The volume of the tandem and multi-axle vehicles has increased manifold and heavier loads are common. Experience has been gained on the use of the new form of construction and materials such as stone matrix asphalt, modified bitumen, foamed bitumen, bitumen emulsion, warm asphalt, cement bases and sub-bases since the last revision of guidelines. Attention is focused on fatigue resistant bituminous mixes with viscosity binders for heavy traffic with a view to construct high performance long life bituminous pavements.

The focus from the use of large scale conventional aggregates is shifted as conventional material like aggregates are becoming progressively scarce as well as legal restrictions on quarrying while the construction activity has expanded phenomenally.

2.2.1 Scope of IRC Guidelines for Flexible Pavements

The guidelines shall apply to the design of new flexible pavements for Expressways, National Highways, and State Highways, Major District Roads and the other categories of roads predominantly carrying motorized vehicles. These guidelines do not form a rigid and sound engineering judgments considering the local environment and past pavement performance in the respective regions should be given due consideration while selecting a pavement composition.

For the purpose of the guidelines, flexible pavements include pavements with bituminous surface with:

- Granular base and sub-base.
- Cement bases and sub-bases with a crack relief layer of aggregate interlayer below the bituminous surfacing.
- Cement bases and sub-bases with SAMI (stress absorbing membrane interlayer) in between bituminous surfacing and the cement base layer for retarding the reflection cracks into the bituminous layer.
- Reclaimed Asphalt Pavement (RAP) with or without addition of fresh aggregates treated with foamed bitumen/bitumen emulsion.

These guidelines are not be straightway applied to overlay design for which IRC: 81-1997 or a more suitable procedure based on evaluation of in situ properties of pavement layers by Falling Weight Deflectometer (FWD) should be used.

The guidelines may require revision from time to time in the light of future developments and experience in the field.

2.2.2 Fatigue Cracking and Rutting as Design Criteria

IRC: 37-2001 was based on a Mechanistic Empirical approach, which considered the design life of pavement to last till the fatigue cracking in bituminous surface extended to 20 per cent of the pavement surface area or rutting in the pavement reached the terminal rutting of 20 mm, whichever happened earlier. The same approach and the criteria are followed in these guidelines as well, except that the cracking and rutting have been restricted to 10 per cent of the area for design traffic exceeding 30 msa. These guidelines aim at pavement design by including alternate materials like cement and reclaimed asphalt materials, and subjecting them to analysis using the software IITPAVE, a modified version of FPAVE.

The Guidelines recommend that the following aspects should be given consideration while designing to achieve better performing pavements:

- Incorporation of design period of more than fifteen years.
- Computation of effective CBR of subgrade for pavement design.
- Use of rut resistant surface layer.
- Use of fatigue resistant bottom bituminous layer.
- Selection of surface layer to prevent top down cracking.
- Use of bitumen emulsion/foamed bitumen treated Reclaimed Asphalt Pavements in base course.
- Design of drainage layer.
- Design of drainage layer.
- Computation of equivalent single axle load considering (a) single axle with single wheel (b) single axle with dual wheels (c) tandem axle and (d) tridem axles.
- Design of perpetual pavements with deep strength bituminous layer.

2.2.3 Traffic

The recommended method considers design traffic in terms of the cumulative number of standard axles (80 kN) to be carried by the pavement during the design life. Axle load spectrum data are required where cement bases are used for evaluating the fatigue damage of such bases for heavy traffic. Following information is needed for estimating design traffic:

- Initial traffic after construction in terms of number of Commercial Vehicles per day (CVPD).
- Traffic growth rate during the design life in percentage.
- Design life in number of year.
- Spectrum of axle load.
- Vehicle Damage Factor (VDF).
- Distribution of commercial traffic over the carriageway.

Only the number of commercial vehicles having weight of 30 kN or more and their axle-loading is considered for the purpose of design of pavement.

Assessment of the present day average traffic should be used on seven-day 24-hour count made in accordance with IRC:9-1972, "Traffic Census on Non-Urban Roads".

Traffic Growth rate

The present day traffic has to be projected for the end of design life at growth rates 'r' estimated by studying and analyzing the following data:

- The past trends of traffic growth; and
- Demand elasticity of traffic with respect to macro-economic parameters (like GDP or SDP) and expected demand due to specific developments and land use changes to take place during design life.

If the data for the annual growth rate of commercial vehicles is not available or if it is less than 5 per cent, a growth rate of 5 per cent should be used (IRC SP:84-2009)

Design Life

The design life is defined in terms of the cumulative number of standard axles in msa that can be carried before a major strengthening, rehabilitation or capacity augmentation of the pavement is necessary.

It is recommended that pavement for National Highways and State Highways should be designed for a minimum life of 15 years. Expressways and Urban Roads may be designed for a longer life of 20 years or higher using innovative design adopting high fatigue bituminous mixes. In the light experience in India and abroad, high volume roads with design traffic greater than 200 msa and perpetual pavement can also be designed using the principles stated in guidelines. For other categories, a design life of 10-15 years may be adopted.

If stage construction is adopted, thickness of granular layer should be provided for the full design period. In the case of cemented bases and sub-bases, stage construction may lead to early failure because of high flexural stresses in the cemented layer and, therefore, not recommended.

Vehicle Damage Factor

The guidelines use Vehicle Damage Factor (VDF) in estimation of cumulative msa for thickness design of pavement.

The vehicle damage factor is a multiplier to convert the number of commercial vehicle of different axle loads and axle configuration into the number of repetitions of standard axle load of magnitude 80 kN. It is defined as equivalent number of standard axle per commercial vehicle. The VDF varies with the vehicle axle configuration and axle loading.

The equations for computing equivalency factor for single, tandem and tridem axles given below should be used for converting different axle load repetitions into equivalent standard load repetitions. Since the VDF values in AASHO Road Test for flexible and rigid pavements are not much different, for heavy duty pavements, the computed VDF values are assumed to be same for bituminous with cemented and granular bases.

Single axle with single wheel on either side $\quad = \quad$ (axle load in kN$/65)^4$

Single axle with dual wheels on either side $\quad = \quad$ (axle load in kN$/80)^4$

Tandem axle with dual wheels on either side $= \quad$ (axle load in kN$/148)^4$

Tridem axle with dual wheels on either side $=$ (axle load in kN$/224)^4$

Distribution of Commercial Traffic Over the Carriageway

Distribution of commercial traffic in each direction and in each lane is required for determining the total equivalent standard axle load applications to be considered in the design. In the absence of adequate and conclusive data, the following distribution may be assumed until more reliable data on placement of commercial vehicles on the carriageway lanes are available:

- **Single-lane roads**

Traffic tends to be more channelized on the single-lane roads than two-lane roads and to allow for this concentration of wheel load repetitions, the design should be based on total number of commercial vehicles in both directions.

- **Two-lane single carriageway roads**

The design should be based on 50 per cent of the total number of commercial vehicles in both directions. If vehicle damage factor in one direction is higher the traffic in the direction of higher VDF is recommended for design.

- **Four-lane Single carriageway roads**

The design should be based on 40 per cent of the total number of commercial vehicles in both directions.

- **Dual carriageway roads**

The design of dual two-lane carriageway roads should be based on 75 per cent of the number of commercial vehicles in each direction. For dual three-lane carriageway and dual four lane carriageway, the distribution factor will be 60 per cent and 45 per cent respectively.

Where there is no significant difference between traffic in each of the two directions, design traffic for each direction may be taken as half of the sum of traffic in both directions. Where significant difference between the two streams exists, pavement thickness in each direction can be different and designed accordingly.

For two-way two-lane roads, pavement thickness should be same for both the lanes even if VDF values are different in different directions and designed for higher VDF. For divided carriageways, each direction may have different thickness of pavement if the axle load patterns are significantly different.

Computation of Design Traffic

The design traffic in terms of cumulative number of standard axle to be carried during the design life of the road is calculated using equation 2.1:

$$N = 365 \left[\{(1 + r)^n - 1\}/r \} \right] A\,D\,F \tag{2.1}$$

Where,

N = Cumulative number of standard axles to be catered for in the design in terms of msa

A = Initial traffic in the year of completion of construction in terms of the number of commercial Vehicles per day (CVPD)

D = Lane distribution factor

F = Vehicle Damage Factor

n = Design life in years

r = Annual growth rate of commercial vehicles in decimal (e.g., for 5 per cent annual growth rate, $r = 0.05$)

The traffic in the year of completion is estimated using the following formula:

$$A = P\,(1+r)^x$$

Where,

P = Number of commercial vehicles as per last count

x = Number of year between the last count and the year of completion of construction.

2.2.4 Subgrade

Requirement of CBR for Subgrade

The Subgrade is the top 500 mm of the embankment immediately below the bottom of the pavement, and is made up of in-situ material, select soil, stabilized soil that forms the foundation of a pavement. It should be well compacted to limit the scope of rutting in pavement due to additional densification during the service life of pavement. Subgrade shall be compacted to a minimum of 97 per cent of laboratory dry density achieved with heavy compaction as per IS: 2720 (Part 8) for Expressways, National Highways, State Highways, Major District Road and other heavily trafficked roads.

The select soil forming the subgrade should have a minimum CBR of 8 per cent for roads having traffic of 450 commercial vehicles per day or higher.

Effective CBR

Where there is significant difference between the CBR of the select subgrade and embankment soil, the design should be based on effective CBR which can be determined from Figure 2.1.

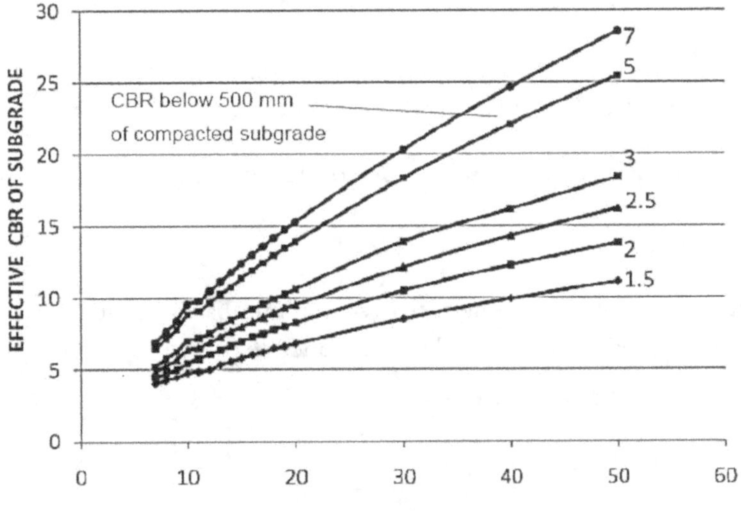

CBR of Compacted Borrow Material 500 mm Thick

Fig 2.1 Effective CBR of Subgrade

In case the borrowed material is placed over the rocky foundation, the effective CBR may be larger than the CBR of the borrow material. Use of the CBR of borrow material may be adopted for pavement design with proper safeguards against development of pore water pressure between the foundation and borrow material.

Determination of Resilient Modulus

Resilient modulus is a measure of elastic behavior of soil determined by recoverable deformations in the laboratory test. The modulus is an important parameter in the design and the performance of pavement. This can be determined in the laboratory by conducting test as per procedure specified AASHTO T307-99(2003). Since the repetitive tri-axial testing facility is not widely available and is expensive, the default resilient modulus can be estimated from generally acceptable correlations:

The relation between resilient modulus and effective CBR (%) is given in equation 2.2.

$$\begin{aligned} M_R \quad &= 10 * CBR \qquad\qquad \text{for CBR} \le 5 \\ &= 17.6 * (CBR)^{0.64} \qquad \text{for CBR} > 5 \end{aligned} \tag{2.2}$$

Where

M_R = Resilient modulus of subgrade soil in MPa

CBR = Effective CBR of subgrade soil in percent

Poisson's Ratio for Subgrade Soil: A value of 0.25 is recommended.

2.2.5 Granular Layer

Granular layer is used to construct Base and Sub-base. Granular layer may consist of crushed stone, crushed slag or concrete or slate.

Resilient Modulus of Granular Layer

$$M_{R\,gsb} = 0.2\, h^{0.45} * M_{R\,subgrade} \tag{2.3}$$

Where,

M_R = Resilient modulus of subgrade soil in MPa

h = Thickness of sub-base layer in mm

Poisson's Ratio of Granular Layer

A value of 0.35 is recommended for bases and sub-bases.

2.2.5 Bituminous Layer

Bituminous layer is top most layer of the flexible pavement and it acts as the binder / wearing course.

Resilient Modulus of Bituminous Layer

Resilient Modulus of Bituminous layer are given in table 2.1.

Table 2.1 Resilient Modulus of Bituminous layer (MPa)

Mix Type	Temperature ^{0}C				
	20	25	30	35	40
Bituminous Concrete (BC) & Dense Bituminous Macadam (DBM) for VG-10 bitumen	2300	2000	1450	1000	800
BC & DBM for VG-30 bitumen	3500	3000	2500	1700	1250
BC & DBM for VG-40 bitumen	6000	5000	4000	3000	2000
BC & DBM for Modified Bitumen	5700	3800	2400	1650	1300
Bituminous Macadam (BM) with VG-10 bitumen	500 MPa at 35°C				
BM with VG-30 bitumen	700 MPa at 35°C				
Wet Mix Macadam (WMM)/ Reclaimed Asphalt Pavement (RAP) treated with 3 per cent bitumen emulsion/foamed bitumen (2 per cent residual bitumen and 1 per cent cementitious material).	600 MPa at 35°C (laboratory values vary from 600 to 1200 MPa for water saturated samples).				

Poisson's Ratio

Poisson's ratio for bituminous layers depends upon the pavement temperature and a value of 0.35 is recommended for temperature up to 35^0C and a value of 0.50 for higher temperatures.

2.2.6 Principles of Pavement Design

Pavement Model

A flexible pavement is modeled as an elastic multilayer structure. The stress analysis software IITPAVE has been used for the computation of stresses and strains in flexible pavements at critical locations due to fatigue and rutting as shown in Figure 2.2 and Figure 2.3.

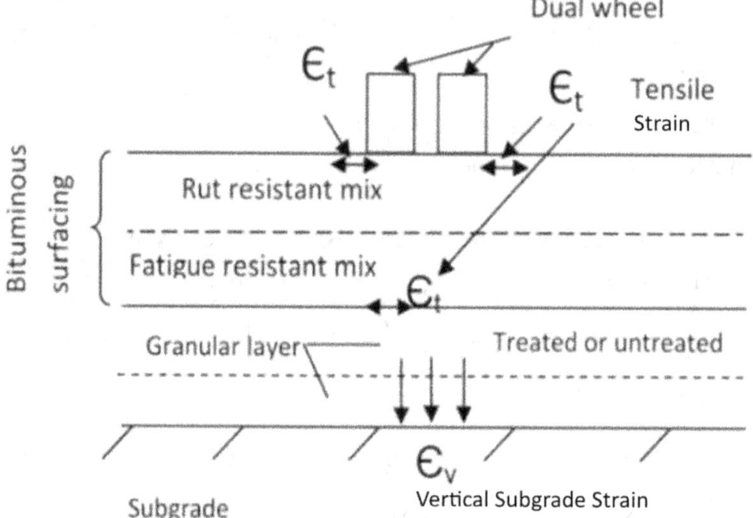

Fig. 2.2 Tensile Strain and Vertical Subgrade Strain

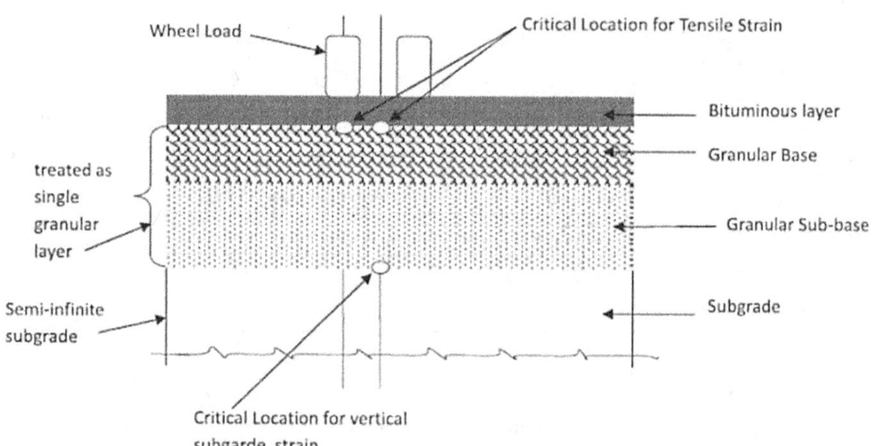

Fig. 2.3 Critical Locations for Tensile Strain and Subgrade Strain

Fatigue Model

Repeated application of traffic loads on the pavement causes tensile strain at the bottom of the bituminous layer. Every load repetition goes on widening and expanding the cracks developed at the bottom of bituminous layers till the cracks propagate to the surface. The phenomenon is known as fatigue. Bituminous surfacing of pavements displays flexural fatigue cracking if the tensile strain at the bottom of bituminous layer is beyond certain limit. The relation between the fatigue life of the pavement and the tensile strain ε_t in the bottom of bituminous layer was obtained as a result of research studies sponsored by Ministry of Road Transport and Highways (MoRTH) of India.

Fatigue model has been calibrated using the pavement performance data collected during these studies. Two fatigue equations were fitted, one in which the computed strains in 80 per cent of the actual data in the scatter plot were higher than the limiting strains predicted by the model (and termed as 80 per cent reliability level) and the other corresponding to 90 percent reliability level. The two equations for the conventional bituminous mixes designed by Marshall method are given as equations 2.4 and 2.5.

$$N_f = 2.21*10^{-04} \times [1/\varepsilon_t]^{3.89} * [1/M_R]^{0.854} \quad (80\% \text{ reliability}) \quad (2.4)$$

$$N_f = 0.711*10^{-04} \times [1/\varepsilon_t]^{3.89} * [1/M_R]^{0.854} \quad (90\% \text{ reliability}) \quad (2.5)$$

Where,

$\quad N_f =$ fatigue life in number of standard axles

$\quad \varepsilon_t =$ maximum tensile strain at bottom of the bituminous layer

$\quad M_R =$ resilient modulus of the bituminous layer

As per the prevailing practice, the mixes used in the pavements under study sections were generally designed for 4.5 per cent air voids (V_a) and bitumen content of 4.5 per cent by weight of the mix (which in terms of volume would come to 11.5 per cent, V_b). Most literature recommend a factor 'C' to be introduced in fatigue models to take into account the effect of air voids (V_a) and volume of bitumen (V_b), which is given by the following relationships:

$$C = 10^M, \quad \text{and} \quad M = 4.84\{V_b/(V_a+V_b)-0.69\}$$

Corresponding to the values of V_a and V_b as stated above, introduction of

'C' in equation (2.5) leads the equation (2.6).

$$N_f = 0.5161 * C * 10^{-04} \times [1/\varepsilon_t]^{3.89} * [1/M_R]^{0.854} \tag{2.6}$$

Rutting Model

Rutting is the permanent deformation in pavement usually occurring longitudinally along the wheel path. It is caused by deformation in subgrade and other non-bituminous layers which reflect in the overlying layers.

The allowable number of load repetitions to control pavement deformation can be expressed as equations (2.7) and (2.8).

Like the fatigue model, rutting model also has been calibrated using the pavement performance data collected during the studies sponsored by MoRTH at 80 per cent and 90 per cent reliability levels. The two equations are given below:

$$N = 4.1656 * 10^{-08} * [1/\varepsilon_v]^{4.5337} \qquad (80\% \text{ reliability}) \tag{2.7}$$

$$N = 1.41 * 10^{-08} * [1/\varepsilon_v]^{4.5337} \qquad (90\% \text{ reliability}) \tag{2.8}$$

Where,

N = Number of cumulative standard axles, and

ε_v = Vertical strain in the Subgrade

The equations for 80% reliability value are adopted for design traffic less than equal to 30 msa and 90% reliability equations are adopted for the design traffic more than 30 msa.

2.3 IRC METHOD FOR DESIGN OF RIGID PAVEMENTS

The method is covered in the guidelines of IRC:58-2015 applicable to design of plain jointed cement concrete pavements with and without tied concrete shoulders. The guidelines are applicable to the roads having average daily traffic volume of more than 450 (vehicles with laden weight exceeding 3 tonne). The main factors governing design are listed below.

2.3.1 Axle Load Characteristics

The legal axle load limits in India are 100 kN, 186 kN, 235 kN for single, tandem and tridem axles respectively. Minimum percentages of commercial vehicles to be weighed should be 10 percent for volume of commercial vehicles per day (CVPD) exceeding 6000, 15 percent for CVPD for 3000 to 6000 and 20 percent for CVPD less than 3000. For most of commercial vehicles, the commonly used tyre inflation pressures range from about 0.7 MPa to 1 MPa. It is found that stresses in concrete pavements having thickness of 200 mm or higher are not affected significantly by variation of tyre pressure. A tyre pressure of 0.8 MPa is adopted for design.

2.3.2 Wheel Base Characteristics

Information on typical spacing between successive axles of commercial vehicles is necessary to identify the proportion of axles that should be considered for estimating top-down cracking caused by axle loads during night period when slab has the tendency of curling up due to negative temperature differential. If the spacing between any pair of axles is less than the spacing of transverse joints, such axles need to be considered in design traffic for computing top-down fatigue cracking damage. The axles with the spacing more than 4.5 m are not expected to contribute to top-down fatigue cracking.

2.3.3 Design Period

Mostly these pavements are designed for 30 years or more. However, the design engineer should use his/her own judgement about the design period taking into consideration factors such as traffic volume, uncertainty of traffic growth rate and capacity of the road.

2.3.4 Traffic Consideration

The lane carrying the maximum number of heavy commercial vehicles is termed as design lane. Each lane of a two-way two-lane highway and outer lane of multi-lane highways can be considered as design lanes.

Annual traffic growth rate of commercial vehicles shall be taken to be minimum 5 percent. The traffic counts and corresponding traffic estimates should indicate the day and night traffic trends as the loading during the day hours is generally responsible for bottom-up cracking whereas the night time traffic may lead to top-down cracking. It is recommended that 25 percent of the total two-way commercial traffic may be considered as design traffic for two-lane two-way roads for the bottom-up cracking. In the case of four lane and other multilane divided highways, 25 percent of the total traffic in the direction of predominant traffic may be considered for design of pavement for the bottom-up cracking.

The design cumulative number of axle load repetitions for fatigue damage can be obtained from the cumulative number of commercial vehicles as given below in Equation (2.9).

$$C = 365 \times A \times \{(1+r)^n - 1\}/r \qquad \qquad \dots\dots\dots\dots(2.9)$$

Where

C = Cumulative number of commercial vehicles during the design period

A = Initial number of commercial vehicles per day in the year when road is opened to traffic

r = Annual rate of growth of commercial traffic volume (expressed as decimal)

n = Design period in years

Table 2.2 Temperature Differentials for Concrete Slab in India

Zone	States/Regions	Max. Temperature Differential (^{0}C) in CC Slab of thickness			
		150 mm	200 mm	250 mm	300-400 mm
1	Hilly region UK, West Bengal, J&K,HP and AP	12.5	13.5	14.3	15.8
2	Punjab, UP, UK, Gujarat, Rajasthan, Haryana and North MP excluding hilly regions	12.5	13.1	14.3	15.8
3	Bihar, Jharkhand, West Bengal, Assam and Eastern Orissa excluding hilly regions and coastal areas	15.6	16.4	16.6	16.8
4	Maharashtra, Karnataka, South MP, Chhattisgarh, AP, Western Orissa and North Tamil Nadu excluding hilly regions and coastal areas	17.3	19.0	20.3	21.0
5	Kerala and South Tamil Nadu, excluding hilly regions and coastal areas	15.0	16.4	17.6	18.1
6	Coastal areas bounded by hills	14.6	15.8	16.2	17.0
7	Coastal areas unbounded by hills	15.5	17.0	19.0	19.2

2.3.5 Temperature Consideration

Temperature differential between top and bottom fibres of concrete pavements causes the concrete slab to curl, giving rise to stresses. The temperature differential is a function of solar radiation received by the pavement surface, wind velocity and thermal diffusivity of concrete. In the absence of any local data, the maximum temperature differential values given in Table 2.2 may be adopted for pavement design.

Temperature differentials are positive when the slab has the tendency to have a convex shape during the day hours and negative with concave shape during the night. Since it is too cumbersome to carry out hourly cumulative damage analysis, it is suggested that the maximum positive and negative temperature differentials respectively assumed to be constant for six hour period during the day between 10 AM to 4 PM and for six hour period between 0 AM to 6 AM during the night hours. The slab may be assumed to be free of warping stresses for the remaining 12 hours for the purpose of fatigue damage analysis as the fatigue damage caused by the combined action of load and temperature differential will be insignificant during this period.

2.3.6 Embankment Soil and Characteristics of Subgrade and Sub base

CBR of embankment soil placed below the 500 mm select subgrade should be determined for estimating the effective CBR of subgrade and its 'k' value for design. The nature of embankment strata such as expansive clays, marine clays, soft clays, black cotton soil etc. needs to be studied to take the special measures like consolidation of strata by accelerated pore pressure dissipation, removal of expansive black cotton soil strata and replacement by non-expansive, use of geo synthetics to arrest tension cracks or soil stabilization etc. Expansive soils should be compacted at 1-3 percent above optimum moisture content (OMC) as determined by modified proctor compaction.

The subgrade is usually considered as a Winkler foundation, also known as dense liquid foundation. The strength of subgrade is expressed in terms of modulus of subgrade reaction, k which is defined as the pressure per unit deflection of the foundation as determined by plate load tests. The k-value is determined from the pressure sustained at a deflection of 1.25 mm. IS 9214-1974 may be referred to for the guidance in this regard.

The subgrade soil strength and consequently the strength of the foundation as a whole, is affected by its moisture content. Since the k-value cannot be determined in the field at different moisture contents and densities, CBR tests may be carried out at field moisture content and field density in soaked and un-soaked condition. The plate load test is time consuming and expensive and therefore, the design k-value is often estimated from soaked CBR value. The relationship between the CBR and k-value is illustrated in Table 2.3 and Table 2.4 shows the k-values for dry lean concrete sub-base.

Table 2.3 k-Value and CBR value for Soil Subgrade in India

Soaked CBR (%)	k-value (MPa/m)	Soaked CBR (%)	k-value (MPa/m)
2	21	10	55
3	28	15	62
4	35	20	69
5	42	50	140
7	48	100	220

Table 2.4 k-Values for Dry Lean Concrete Sub-base in India

k-value of subgrade (MPa/m)	Effective k for 100 mm DLC, (MPa/m)	Effective k for 150 mm DLC, (MPa/m)
21	56	97
28	97	138
42	166	208
48	208	277
55	278	300
62	300	300

*Note: The above k-value is extrapolated from AASHTO-1993. The maximum recommended value is 300 MPa/m.

The main purpose of the sub-base is to provide a uniform, stable and permanent support to the concrete pavement laid over it. It should have 7-day average compressive strength of 10 MPa determined as per IRC-SP: 49. Minimum recommended thickness of DLC for major highways is 150 mm.

2.3.7 Concrete Properties

Flexural strength of concrete is required for the purpose of design of concrete pavement. It can be derived from characteristic compressive strength of concrete as per IS 456-2000 using Equation (2.10).

$$F_{cr} = 0.7 \times (f_{ck})^{0.5} \qquad \qquad \text{...... (2.10)}$$

Where,

Fcr = Flexural strength (modulus of rupture), MPa

fck = Characteristic compressive strength of concrete, MPa

Usually, concrete design is based on 28 days strength. But in case of concrete pavement, 90 days strength can be permitted in view of the fact that during initial period of 90 days, the number of repetitions of load is very small and has negligible effect on cumulative fatigue damage of concrete. Increasing the 28 days flexural strength by a factor 1.1 is recommended to get 90 days strength. In no case 28 days flexural strength of pavement quality concrete should be less than 4.5 MPa.

The elastic modulus increases with increase in strength and Poisson's ratio decreases with increase in the modulus of elasticity. Generally a value of modulus of elasticity, E is taken as 30,000 MPa and Poisson's ratio is taken as 0.15.

Coefficient of thermal expansion of concrete is dependent to a great extent on the type of aggregates used in concrete. However, for design purpose, a value of α = 10 x 10-6 per o C is adopted. Due to repeated application of flexural stresses by the traffic loads, progressive fatigue damage takes place in the concrete pavement in the form of gradual development of micro-cracks especially when ratio between the applied flexural stress and the flexural strength of concrete is high. This ratio is termed as stress ratio (SR). The relation between fatigue life (N) and SR is given below in Equation (2.11), (2.12), (2.13).

$$N = \text{unlimited for SR} < 0.45 \qquad \qquad \text{.....(2.11)}$$

$$N = \{4.2577/(SR-0.4325)\}^{3.268} \qquad \text{For } 0.45 \leq SR \leq 0.55 \qquad \text{.....(2.12)}$$

$$\log N = (0.9718-SR)/0.0828 \qquad \text{For } SR > 0.55 \qquad \text{.....(2.13)}$$

2.3.8 Design of Slab Thickness

The flexural stress due to combined action of traffic loads and temperature differential between the top and bottom fibres of concrete slab is considered for design of pavement thickness. Location of maximum tensile stress on concrete slab in mid-day and night hours is shown in Fig. 2.4 and Fig. 2.5 respectively. Figure 2.6 and 2.7 show the placement of axles on the slab for causing the maximum stress.

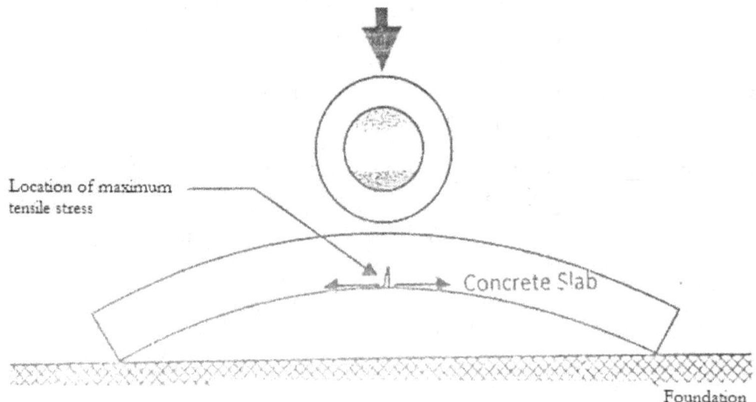

Fig. 2.4 Axle Load Placed in middle of the Slab during Mid-Day

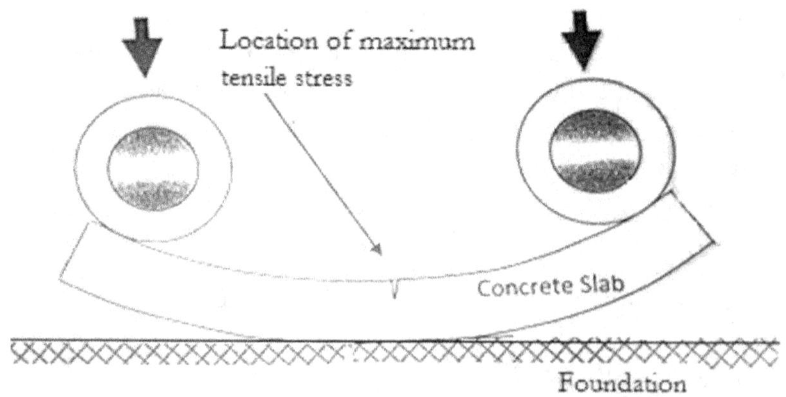

Fig. 2.5 Placement of Two Axles of a Commercial Vehicle on a Slab Curled during Night Hours

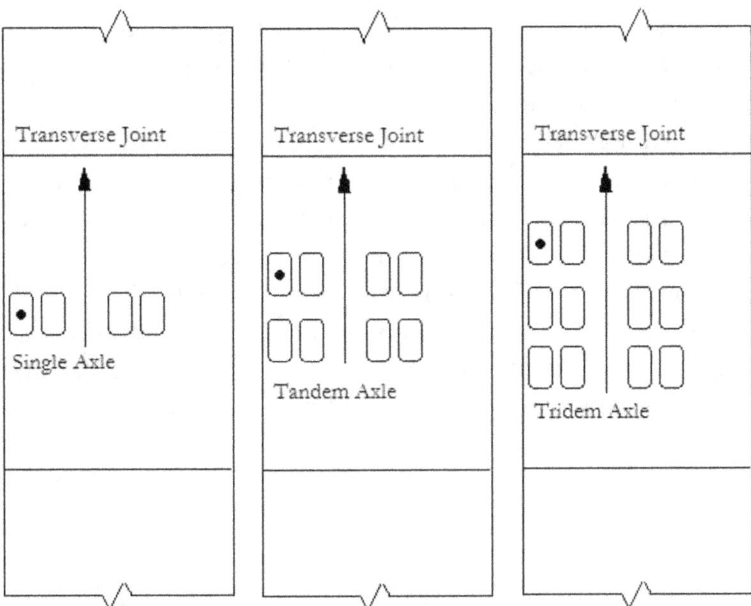

Fig. 2.6 Placement of Axles for Maximum Edge Flexural Stress at Bottom of the Slab

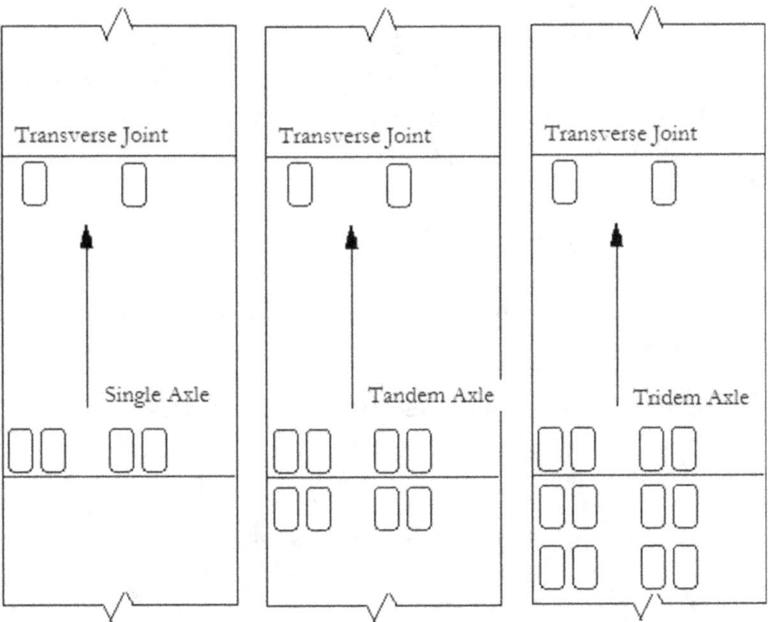

Fig. 2.7 Different Axle Load Positions Causing Tensile Stress at Top of the Slab

Tied concrete shoulders are also necessary for high volume pavements. But for the traffic volumes smaller than 450 CVPD tied concrete shoulders and dowel bars are not generally warranted.

For a given pavement thickness and other design parameters, the pavement will be checked for cumulative bottom-up and top-down fatigue damage that will cause bottom up cracking (BUC) and top down cracking (TDC) respectively in the slab. The cumulative fatigue damage caused to the slab due to BUC and TDC during its service life collectively should be equal to or less than one. The cumulative fatigue damage (CFD) expressions for bottom-up and top-down cracking cases are shown in Equation 2.14 and Equation 2.15.

$$\text{CFD(BUC)} = \sum_{i}^{j} \frac{ni}{Ni} \quad \text{(10 AM to 4 PM)} \tag{2.14}$$

$$\text{CFD(TDC)} = \sum_{i}^{j} \frac{ni}{Ni} \quad \text{(0 AM to 6 AM)} \tag{2.15}$$

Where

Ni = Allowable number of load and temperature differential cycles for the wheel load group during the specified six-hour period

ni = Predicted number of load and temperature differential cycles for the ith load group during the specified six-hour period

j = Total number of load group

2.3.9 Regression Equations for Flexural Stress in Concrete Slab

Expressions for maximum tensile stress at the bottom of the slab (<u>BUC case</u>)

Single axle – Pavement with tied concrete shoulders

(a) $k \leq 80$ MPa/m

$$S = 0.008 - 6.12(\gamma h^2/k\ell^2) + 2.36(Ph/k\ell^4) + 0.0266\Delta T \tag{2.16}$$

(b) $k > 80$ MPa/m, $k \leq 150$ MPa/m

$$S = 0.08 - 9.69(\gamma h^2/k\ell^2) + 2.09(Ph/k\ell^4) + 0.0409\Delta T \tag{2.17}$$

(c) $k > 150$ MPa/m

$$S = 0.042 + 3.26(\gamma h^2/k\ell^2) + 1.62(Ph/k\ell^4) + 0.0522\Delta T \qquad (2.18)$$

Single axle – Pavement without tied concrete shoulders

(a) $k \leq 80$ MPa/m

$$S = -0.149 - 2.60(\gamma h2/k\ell2) + 3.13(Ph/k\ell4) + 0.0297\Delta T \qquad (2.19)$$

(b) $k > 80$ MPa/m, $k \leq 150$ MPa/m

$$S = -0.119 - 2.99(\gamma h^2/k\ell^2) + 2.78(Ph/k\ell^4) + 0.0456\Delta T \qquad (2.20)$$

(c) $k > 150$ MPa/m

$$S = -0.238 + 7.02(\gamma h^2/k\ell^2) + 2.41(Ph/k\ell^4) + 0.0585\Delta T \qquad (2.21)$$

Tandem axle – Pavement with tied concrete shoulders

(a) $k \leq 80$ MPa/m

$$S = -0.188 + 0.93(\gamma h^2/k\ell^2) + 1.025(Ph/k\ell^4) + 0.0207\Delta T \qquad (2.22)$$

(b) $k > 80$ MPa/m, $k \leq 150$ MPa/m

$$S = -0.174 + 1.21(\gamma h^2/k\ell^2) + 0.87(Ph/k\ell^4) + 0.0364\Delta T \qquad (2.23)$$

(c) $k > 150$ MPa/m

$$S = -0.210 + 3.88(\gamma h^2/k\ell^2) + 0.73(Ph/k\ell^4) + 0.0506\Delta T \qquad (2.24)$$

Tandem axle – Pavement without tied concrete shoulders

(a) $k \leq 80$ MPa/m

$$S = -0.223 + 2.73(\gamma h^2/k\ell^2) + 1.335(Ph/k\ell^4) + 0.0229\Delta T \qquad (2.25)$$

(b) $k > 80$ MPa/m, $k \leq 150$ MPa/m

$$S = -0.276 + 5.78(\gamma h^2/k\ell^2) + 1.14(Ph/k\ell^4) + 0.0404\Delta T \qquad (2.26)$$

(c)   k >150 MPa/m

$$S = -0.3 + 9.88(\gamma h^2/k\ell^2) + 0.965(Ph/k\ell^4) + 0.0543\Delta T \qquad (2.27)$$

Expressions for maximum tensile stress at the top of the slab (TDC case)

For analysis of top-down cracking, only rear axle load is input. Front axle load is assumed to be 50% of rear axle load (tandem/tridem).

$$S = -0.219 + 1.686B(Ph/k\ell^4) + 168.48(h^2/k\ell^2) + 0.1089\Delta T \qquad (2.28)$$

The symbols in the equation have following meaning.

S = flexural stress in slab, MPa

ΔT = maximum temperature differential in ℃ during day time for bottom-up cracking

= sum of maximum night time negative temperature differential and built-in negative temperature differential in ℃ for top - down cracking

h = thickness of slab, m

k = effective modulus of subgrade reaction of foundation, MPa/m

l = radius of relative stiffness = $[Eh^3/\{12k(1-\mu^2)\}]^{0.25}$

E = elastic modulus of concrete, MPa

μ = Poisson's ratio of concrete

γ = unit weight of concrete (24 kN/m³)

P = for bottom-up cracking analysis: single/tandem rear axle load (kN). No fatigue damage computed for front (steering) axles for bottom-up cracking case.

= for top-down cracking analysis: 100% of rear single axle, 50% of rear tandem axle, and 33% of rear tridem axle. No front axle weight is required to be given as input for top-down cracking case in Equation 3.20. 50% of rear single axle, 25% of rear tandem axle, 16.5% of rear tridem axle, has been considered in the finite element analysis as the front axle weights for single, tandem and tridem rear axles respectively.

B = 0.66 for transverse joint with dowel bar (load transfer efficiency taken as 50%)

= 0.90 for transverse joint without dowel bar (load transfer efficiency taken as 10%)

2.3.10 Tied Concrete Shoulder and Widened Outer Lane

Tied cement concrete shoulders are recommended to protect the edge region of high volume pavements. Widening of outer lanes of pavements by 0.5 m to 0.6 m can be adopted for pavements to reduce the flexural stresses in the wheel path region. Thicknesses of pavements with widened outer lane as well as tied concrete shoulder are almost same.

2.3.11 Design of Joints

Great care is needed in the design and construction of joints in cement concrete pavements, as these are critical locations having significant effect on the pavement performance. The joints also need to be effectively sealed and maintained well. Mainly pavements have transverse and longitudinal joints. Different types of transverse joints are:

1. Contraction joints are transverse joints which relieve the tensile stresses in concrete pavement. The spacing of contraction joints should be limited to 4.5 m to prevent top-down cracking during the night hours.
2. Expansion joints are provided near permanent structure like bridges and culverts.
3. Contraction joints are placed at the location of contraction joints except in case of emergency when a key joint may be used.
4. Longitudinal joints are required in concrete pavements of width greater than 4.5 m to allow for transverse contraction and warping.

2.3.12 Design of Dowel Bars and Tie Bars

Dowels bars enable good riding quality to be maintained by preventing faulting at the joints. For general provisions in respect of dowels bars, stipulations laid down in IRC: 15, may be followed. Detail of dowel bars and tie bars is shown in Table 3.4 and Table 3.5 respectively. The bearing stress in the concrete pavements is responsible for the performance of dowel bars at the joints. Maximum bearing stress (F_{bmax}) between concrete and dowel bar is obtained from this Equation (2.29).

$$F_{bmax} = k_{mds}P_t(2+\beta Z)/(4\beta^3 EI) \tag{2.29}$$

Where

β $\quad$ = $\quad$ Relative stiffness of the bar embedded in concrete, mm^{-1}

$\quad\quad$ = $\quad$ $\{k_{mds}b_d/(4EI)\}^{0.25}$

k_{mds} $\quad$ = $\quad$ Modulus of dowel support, MPa/m

b $\quad$ = $\quad$ Diameter of dowel, mm

z $\quad$ = $\quad$ Joint width (5 mm for contraction joint and 20 mm for expansion joint), in mm

E $\quad$ = $\quad$ Modulus of the elasticity of the dowel bar, MPa

I $\quad$ = $\quad$ Moment of inertia of the dowel, mm^4

Pt $\quad$ = $\quad$ Load transferred by design dowel bar, kN

The modulus of dowel support ranges from 80,000 to 4,15,000 MPa/m. A typical value of 415000 MPa/m may be adopted for design as only the fourth root of this value affects the computation of β. Each dowel bar should be designed for the maximum load being transferred by it for the allowable bearing pressure. Equation (2.30) given by American Concrete Institute (ACI) Committee-225 may be used for calculations of the allowable bearing stress on concrete.

$$F_b \quad = \quad (101.6\text{-}b_d)f_{ck}/95.25 \tag{2.30}$$

Where,

F_b $\quad$ = $\quad$ Allowable bearing stress, MPa

b_d $\quad$ = $\quad$ Dowel diameter, mm

f_{ck} $\quad$ = $\quad$ Characteristic compressive strength of concrete, MPa

$\quad\quad\quad$ For M40 concrete, fck $\quad$ = 40 MPa (28 days)

$\quad\quad\quad\quad\quad\quad\quad\quad\quad\quad\quad$ = 48 MPa (90 days)

Table 2.5 gives the values of the dowel bar details that are used for 4.5 m x 3.5 m size (length x width) rigid pavement slabs for concrete roads in India. Dowel bars are not satisfactory for slabs of small thickness and shall not be provided for slab of less than 200 mm thickness. It is also recommended that dowel bars shall be provided when traffic on the road is 450 CVPD or higher.

Table 2.5 Recommended Dimensions of Dowel Bars

Slab Thickness mm	Dowel bar details		
	Diameter mm	Length mm	Spacing mm
200	25	360	300
230	30	400	300
250	32	450	300
280	36	450	300
300	38	500	300
350	38	500	300

The longitudinal joint is expected to open up during the service period (in case of heavy traffic, expansive subgrades, etc.) and tie bars may be provided in accordance with recommendation of IRC: 15. The area of steel required per metre length of joint may be computed using equation (2.31).

$$A_s = bfW/S_{st} \tag{2.31}$$

Where,

A_s	=	Area of steel in mm², required per m length of joint
b	=	Lane width in metres
f	=	Coefficient of friction between pavement and sub-base/base (usually taken as 1.5)
W	=	Weight of slab in kN/m²
S_{st}	=	Allowable working stress of steel in MPa

The length of any tie bar should be at least twice that required to develop bond strength equal to working stress of steel. The formula for estimating the length of tie bar is given as Equation (2.32).

$$L = 2\,S_{st}\,A_{cs}\,/\,B\,P_{ptb} \tag{2.32}$$

Where,

L	=	Length of tie bar, mm
S_{st}	=	Allowable working stress of steel in MPa
A_{cs}	=	Cross-sectional area of one tie bar, mm²
P_{ptb}	=	Perimeter of tie bar, mm
B	=	Permissible bond stress of concrete,

for deformed tie bars   = 2.46 MPa, and
for plain tie bars   = 1.75 MPa

Table 2.6 Details of Tie Bars for Longitudinal Joint of Two Lane Rigid Pavements used in India

Slab Thickness mm	Tie bar Details				
	Diameter mm	Max. Spacing, mm		Minimum length, mm	
		Plain	Deformed	Plain	Deformed
150	8	330	530	440	480
	10	250	830	510	560
200	10	390	620	510	560
	12	560	900	580	640
250	12	450	720	580	640
300	12	370	600	580	640
	16	660	1060	720	800
350	12	320	510	580	640
	16	570	910	720	800

Note: Permissible Tensile stress, Sst = 125 MPa for plain bars, 200 MPa for deformed bars; bond stress for plain bars = 1.75 MPa, for deformed bars = 2.46 MPa as per IRC: 15.

2.3.13 Design Steps as per IRC:58-2015 Method

The design steps for the design of a rigid pavement as per IRC:58-2015 are summarized below:

o   Stipulate design values for various parameters as per section 3.2.
o   Decide types and spacing of joints as per Table 3.4 and Table 3.5.
o   Select a trial thickness of pavement slab.
o   Compute the repetition of loads of different magnitude during design period as per section 3.2.4.
o   Calculate stresses due to single and tandem axle load by BUC and TDC analyses and determine cumulative fatigue damage (CFD) using Equation (3.6) and Equation (3.7).
o   If CFD>1, select higher thickness and repeat all above 5 steps.
o   Provide dowel bars if traffic at the start of the functioning of the pavement is more than 450 CVPD.
o   Finally design of joints done as per section 2.3.11 and 2.3.12.

3   DESIGN OF PAVEMENT

3.1 GENERAL

The equivalent design traffic for rigid pavement has been calculated from the given design traffic of flexible pavement design using the appropriate formulas from IRC:37-2012 and IRC:58-2015 respectively. The calculated design traffic values are presented in table 3.1. The design of flexible and rigid pavements has been done for these design traffic values and equivalent traffic values respectively.

Table 3.1 Design Traffic for 15 years design life

Flexible Pavement (msa)	Rigid Pavement			
	No. of Axles in both directions (msa)	Lateral Distribution Factor	Design msa for BUC	Design msa for TDC
2	2	0.25	0.1041741	0.085943633
5	5		0.26099525	0.215321081
10	10		0.52199055	0.430642204
20	21		1.0451012	0.86220849
30	31		1.5659716	1.29192657
50	52		2.61107285	2.154135101
100	104		5.22214565	4.308270161
150	157		7.8332185	6.462405263

3.2 DESIGN OF FLEXIBLE PAVEMENT

3.2.1 General

Indian Roads Congress has specified the design procedures for flexible pavements based on CBR values. The pavement designs given in the previous edition IRC: 37-1984 were applicable to design traffic up to only 30 million standard axles (msa). The earlier code was empirical in nature which had limitations regarding applicability and extrapolation. The latest guidelines follow mechanistic empirical designs and developed new set of designs up to 150 msa in IRC: 37-2012.

3.2.2 Design Criteria

A flexible pavement is modeled as an elastic multilayer structure. Stresses and strains at critical locations are computed using a linear layered elastic model. To give proper consideration to the aspects of performance, the following three types of pavement distress resulting from repeated (cyclic) applicable of traffic loads are considered:

(i)   Vertical compressive strain at the top of the subgrade which can cause subgrade deformation resulting in permanent deformation at the pavement surface.

(ii) Horizontal tensile strain or stress at the bottom of the bituminous layer which can cause fracture of the bituminous layer.

(iii) Pavement deformation within the bituminous layer.

While the permanent deformation within the bituminous layer can be controlled meeting the mix design requirements, thickness of granular and bituminous layer is selected using the analytical design approach so that strains at the critical points as shown in Figure 2.3 are within the allowable limits. For calculating tensile strains at bottom of the bituminous layer VG-30 grade bitumen has been used in present analysis.

3.2.3 Fatigue Criteria

Centre of the dual wheels and centre of the outer wheel beneath the bituminous layer of the pavement are the two critical locations for tensile strain (ε_t) as shown in Figure 2.3. Maximum value of the strain is adopted for the design. Similarly, centre of the dual wheels over the subgrade is the critical location for the vertical subgrade strain (ε_z) since the maximum value of the ε_z occurs at this point.

Bituminous surfacing of pavement displays flexural fatigue cracking if the tensile strain at the bottom of bituminous layer is beyond certain limit. The relation between the fatigue life of the pavement and the tensile strain in the bottom of the bituminous layer is obtained by equations (2.4) and (2.5).

3.2.4 Rutting Criteria

The allowable number of load repetitions to control permanent deformation can be found using equations (2.7) and (2.8).

3.2.5 Design Procedure

Based on the performance of existing designs and using analytical approach, simple design charts are added in the IRC code in the form of plates. The pavement designs are given for subgrade CBR values ranging from 4% to 10% and design traffic 2 msa to 150 msa. The later thickness obtained from the following simple input parameters, appropriate design traffic and CBR value of subgrade.

3.2.6 Design for the Given Data

Design Traffic: 2 msa, Subgrade CBR: 4%, Design Life: 15 years

Step-1: Thickness of pavement layers

From plate 2 corresponding to CBR of 4% and traffic 2 msa

SDBC (Semi Dense Bituminous Concrete)	=	20 mm
DBM (Dense Bituminous Macadam)	=	50 mm
WMM (Wet Mix Macadam)	=	225 mm
GSB (Granular Subbase)	=	265mm

Step-2: Computation of allowable strains

Allowable Horizontal tensile strain, ε_t

$$N_f = 2.21*10^{-04} \times [1/\varepsilon_t]^{3.89} * [1/M_R]^{0.854}$$

$$M_R = 1700 \text{ at } 35^0C \text{ and for VG-30 Grade Bitumen, and}$$

$$N_f = 2 \text{ msa}$$

$$\varepsilon_t = 526*10^{-6}$$

Allowable Vertical strain, ε_v

$$N = 4.1656*10^{-8}[1/\varepsilon_v]^{4.5337} \qquad \text{where } N = 2 \text{ msa}$$

$$\varepsilon_v = 756*10^{-6}$$

Step-3: Resilient Modulus & Poisson's Ratio

Using equations (2.2) and (2.3)

$M_{R\ Subgrade}$ (MPa)	$= 10*CBR$	= 40 MPa
$M_{R\ Granular}$ (MPa)	$= 0.2*h^{0.45}*M_{R\_Subgrade}$	= 130 MPa
Poisson's ratio of Bituminous Layer		= 0.4
Poisson's ratio of Granular Layer		= 0.35
Poisson's ratio of Subgrade Layer		= 0.25

Step-4: Computation of actual strains using IITPAVE software

Table 3.2 Actual Strain Values from IITPAVE

```
No. of layers            3
E values (MPa)        1700.00  130.00   40.00
Mu values                0.400.350.20
thicknesses (mm)        70.00  490.00
single wheel load (N) 20500.00
tyre pressure (MPa)      0.56
Dual  Wheel
   Z      R     SigmaZ      SigmaT      SigmaR      TaoRZ       DispZ      epZ        epT        epR
  70.00   0.00-0.2626E+00 0.1190E+01 0.9976E+00-0.1794E-01 0.8818E+00-0.6692E-03 0.5271E-03 0.3686E-03
  70.00L  0.00-0.2626E+00-0.4417E-01-0.5944E-01-0.1794E-01 0.8818E+00-0.1741E-02 0.5271E-03 0.3686E-03
  70.00 150.00-0.1707E+00 0.6601E+00-0.1922E+00-0.1100E+00 0.8736E+00-0.2105E-03 0.4737E-03-0.2282E-03
  70.00L 150.00-0.1707E+00-0.3358E-01-0.1012E+00-0.1100E+00 0.8736E+00-0.9504E-03 0.4737E-03-0.2282E-03
 490.00   0.00-0.3260E-01 0.2371E-01 0.1866E-01-0.9198E-02 0.5526E+00-0.3648E-03 0.2199E-03 0.1674E-03
```

Maximum Horizontal Tensile Strain = 0.4737E-03
Maximum Vertical Compressive Strain = -0.3648E-03

3.3 DESIGN OF RIGID PAVEMENT

A rigid pavement for two lane carriageway with tied concrete shoulders has been designed for varying traffic volume and subgrade strength using IRC:58-2015.

3.3.1 Design Parameters

Traffic Data

The traffic on the road mainly consists of:
(i)   Single Axle Vehicles
(ii) Tandem Axle vehicles
(iii) Tridem Axle vehicles

Table 3.3 Axle load spectrum

Single axle		Tandem axle		Tridem axle	
Axle load class (kN)	Frequency (%of axles)	Axle load class(KN)	Frequency (%of axles)	Axle load class(KN)	Frequency (%of axles)
185-195	18.15	380-400	14.5	530-560	5.23
175-185	17.43	360-380	10.5	500-530	4.85
165-175	18.27	340-360	3.63	470-500	3.44
155-165	12.98	320-340	2.5	440-470	7.12
145-155	2.98	300-320	2.69	410-440	10.11
135-145	1.62	280-300	1.26	380-410	12.01
125-135	2.62	260-280	3.9	350-380	15.57
115-125	2.65	240-260	5.19	320-350	13.28
105-115	2.65	220-240	6.3	290-320	4.55
95-105	3.25	200-220	6.4	260-290	3.16
85-95	3.25	180-200	8.9	230-260	3.1
<85	14.15	<180	34.23	<230	17.58
	100		100		100

Design Data

No of lanes	2
Design life **(years)**	15
Transverse Joint spacing **(m)**	4.5
Lane Width **(m)**	3.75

Table 3.4 Percentage contribution of different types of Axles

Axle Type	%
Front single (steering)	0.45
Rear Single	0.15
Rear Tandem	0.25
Rear Tridem	0.15

% of traffic in terms of **msa** with Spacing between front axle & first rear axle < 4.5m = 55%

% of traffic in terms of **msa** during night hours (6PM to 6AM) = 60%

3.3.2 Design of Slab Thickness

Selection of modulus of subgrade reaction

Effective CBR of compacted subgrade in percent = 4.0 %

Modulus of subgrade reaction = 35 MPa/m

Thickness of Granular Sub Base = 150 mm

Thickness of DLC Sub-base with min 7 day compressive strength
of 10 MPa = 150 mm

Effective Modulus of subgrade reaction of combined subgrade +
granular sub base and DLC sub base = 173 MPa/m

Selection of flexural strength of concrete

28 day compressive strength of cement concrete = 40 MPa

90 day compressive strength of cement concrete = 48 MPa

28 day flexural strength of cement concrete = 4.4 MPa

90 day flexural strength of cement concrete = = 4.9 MPa

Selection of Design Traffic for Fatigue Analysis

Total two way commercial vehicles = 886588

Average no. of axles per commercial vehicle = 2.35

No of axles in predominant direction = 2083482

Lateral Distribution Factor = 0.25

Design traffic after adjusting for lateral placement of axles
= 520871

Night time (12 hour) design axle repetitions = 312522

Day time (12 hour) design axle repetitions = 208348

Day time Six Hour Axle Load repetitions (10 AM to 4 PM)
= 104174

Design no of axle loads for **Bottom Up Cracking Analysis (BUC)**
= 104174

Nigh time Six Hour Axle Load Repetitions (0 AM to 6 AM)
= 156261

% of design traffic with spacing between front axle & first rear axle
< 4.5 m = 0.55

Six hour night time design axle load repetitions for
Top Down Cracking Analysis (TDC) (wheel base< 4.5m)
= 85944

Table 3.5 Axle load category-wise for design

Axle Category	Proportion of the Axle Category	Category Wise Axle Rep for BUC Analysis	Category Wise Axle Rep for TDC
Front(steering) single	0.45	46878	38675
Rear Single	0.15	15626	12892
Tandem	0.25	26044	21486
Tridem	0.15	15626	12892

Cumulative Fatigue Damage Analysis (CFD) for BUC and TDC and Selection of Slab Thickness

Effective modulus of subgrade reaction of foundation, k =173 MPa/m

Elastic modulus of concrete, E $= 30,000$ MPa

Poisson's Ratio of concrete $= 0.15$

Unit Weight of concrete $= 24 \text{ kN/m}^3$

Design flexural strength of concrete $= 4.9$ MPa

Max day time Temperature differential in slab (BUC) $= 15.8 \,^0\text{C}$

Night time Temperature differential in slab (TDC) $= 12.9 \,^0\text{C}$

Assumed thickness of slab $= 0.23$ m

Table 3.6 Cumulative Fatigue Damage Analysis for BUC

Rear Single Axles				
Expected Rep (ni)	Flex Stress MPa	Stress Ratio (SR)	Allowed Rep (Ni)	Fatigue Damage (ni/Ni)
2836	3.198	0.646	8581	0.331
2723	3.078	0.622	16814	0.162
2855	2.959	0.598	32947	0.087
2028	2.839	0.574	64561	0.031
466	2.719	0.549	126822	0.004
253	2.599	0.525	270654	0.001
409	2.479	0.501	727484	0.001
414	2.360	0.477	3023255	0.000
414	2.240	0.453	40021040	0

508	2.120	0.428	Infinite	0
508	2.001	0.404	Infinite	0
2211	1.881	0.380	Infinite	0
15626	Fatigue damage from single axles =			0.616

Table 3.6 Cumulative Fatigue Damage Analysis for BUC

Rear Tandem Axles				
Expected Rep(ni)	Flex Stress Mpa	Stress Ratio (SR)	Allowed Rep (Ni)	Fatigue Damage (ni/Ni)
3776	2.761	0.558	100105	0.038
2735	2.653	0.536	188732	0.015
945.	2.545	0.514	408960	0.002
651	2.438	0.492	1128372	0.001
701	2.329	0.471	4956571	0
328	2.221	0.449	Infinite	0
1016	2.113	0.427	Infinite	0
1352	2.006	0.405	Infinite	0
1641	1.898	0.383	Infinite	0
1667	1.790	0.362	Infinite	0
2318	1.682	0.340	Infinite	0
8915	1.574	0.318	Infinite	0
26044	Fatigue Damage from Tandem axles =			0.056

Table 3.7 Cumulative Fatigue Damage Analysis for TDC

Rear Single Axle				
Expected Rep (ni)	Flex Stress Mpa	Stress Ratio (SR)	Allowed Rep (Ni)	Fatigue Damage (ni/Ni)
2340	2.870	0.580	54245	0.043
2247	2.788	0.563	86106	0.026
2355	2.705	0.547	137211	0.018
1673	2.623	0.530	229528	0.007
384	2.541	0.513	422822	0.001
209	2.459	0.497	896919	0
338	2.376	0.480	2386145	0

342	2.294	0.463	9706176	0
342	2.212	0.447	Infinite	0
419	2.130	0.430	Infinite	0
419	2.048	0.414	Infinite	0
1824	1.965	0.397	Infinite	0
12892	Fatigue damage from single axles =			0.095

Table 3.7 Cumulative Fatigue Damage Analysis for TDC

Rear Tandem Axle

Expected Rep (ni)	Flex Stress Mpa	Stress Ratio (SR)	Allowable Rep(Ni)	Fatigue damage (ni/Ni)
3115	2.911	0.588	43055	0.0724
2256	2.829	0.571	68344	0.033
780	2.747	0.555	108485	0.007
537	2.664	0.538	175679	0.003
578	2.582	0.522	307118	0.002
271	2.500	0.505	602673	0
838	2.418	0.488	1410522	0
1115	2.335	0.472	4465995	0
1354	2.253	0.455	26919187	0
1375	2.171	0.439	Infinite	0
1912	2.089	0.422	Infinite	0
7355	2.006	0.405	Infinite	0
21486	Fatigue Damage from tandem axles=			0.119

Rear Tridem Axle

Expected Rep (ni)	Flex Stress Mpa	Stress Ratio (SR)	Allowed Rep (Ni)	Fatigue Damage (ni/Ni)
674	2.801	0.566	79724	0.008
625	2.719	0.549	126865	0.005
443	2.634	0.532	209443	0.002
918	2.555	0.516	378746	0.002
1303	2.472	0.499	781324	0.002
1548	2.390	0.483	1983537	0.001
2007	2.308	0.466	7337597	0

1712	2.226	0.450	Infinite	0
587	2.143	0.433	Infinite	0
407	2.061	0.416	Infinite	0
400	1.979	0.400	Infinite	0
2266	1.897	0.383	Infinite	0
12892	Fatigue damage from tridem axles =			0.021

Cumulative Fatigue Damage Values for Different Trial Thickness

Table 3.8 Cumulative Fatigue Damage Values for Different Trial Thickness

Slab Thickness h, m	CFD for BUC case			CFD for TDC case				Total CFD for BUC + TDC	Remarks
	Rear single axles	Tandem Axle	Total CFD	Rear single axles	Tandem Axles	Rear Tride axles	Total CFD		
0.23	0.616	0.056	0.672	0.095	0.119	0.021	0.234	0.905	Safe
0.22	1.921	0.165	2.086	0.205	0.266	0.046	0.517	2.603	Unsafe
0.21	7.108	0.565	7.674	0.494	0.667	0.107	1.269	8.944	Unsafe
0.20	32.34	2.334	34.67	1.367	1.933	0.277	3.578	38.256	Unsafe

3.3.3 Design of Dowel Bars

Slab Thickness, h	= 230 mm
Joint width, z for expansion joint	= 20 mm
Joint width, z for contraction joint	= 8 mm
Modulus of subgrade reaction, k	= 173 MPa/m
Radius of relative stiffness, ℓ	= 651 mm
E for dowel bar	= 200000 MPa
Modulus of dowel support, k_{mds}	= 415000 MPa/m
Maximum single axle load	= 190 kN
Maximum single wheel load	= 95 kN

Load transfer to the tied concrete shoulders	= 30 %
Wheel load to be considered for dowel design	= 66.5 kN
Safety of dowel bar can be examined for a load	= 80 kN
Percentage of load transfer through dowel bar	= 40 %
Characteristic compressive strength of concrete	= 40 MPa
Diameter of dowel bar	= 32 mm
Permissible bearing stress in concrete (Eq. 2.30)	= 29.42 MPa
Spacing between dowel bars	= 250 mm
Distance of first dowel bar from pavement edge	= 150 mm
Length of dowel bar	= 450 mm

Dowel Bars up to a distance of 1.0* radius of relative stiffness (ℓ), from the point of load application are effective in load transfer

Number of Dowel bars participating in load transfer when load is just over the dowel bar close to the edge of the slab $\qquad$ = 3

Check for Bearing Stress

Moment of inertia of dowel	= 51462.44
Relative stiffness of dowel bar embedded in concrete	= 0.023
Bearing stress in dowel bar	= 28.52
Check (safe if less than allowable bearing stress)	= **Safe**

3.3.4 Design of Tie Bars

Slab Thickness	= 0.23 m
Lane Width	= 3.75 m
Coefficient of friction, f	= 1.5
Density of Concrete	= 24 kN/m^3
Allowable tensile stress in plain bars (as per IRC:15)	= 125 MPa
Allowable tensile stress in deformed bars(IRC:15)	= 200 MPa
Allowable bond stress for plain tie bars	= 1.75 MPa
Allowable bond stress for deformed tie bars	= 2.46 MPa

Design of Deformed bars

Select diameter of tie bar, dt	= 12 mm

Cross sectional area of tie bar $= 113.04 \text{ mm}^2$

Area of deformed steel bar required per meter width of joint to resist the frictional force at slab bottom, As (Eq. 2.31) $= 155 \text{ mm}^2$

Spacing of tie bars, $= A/As$ $= 728 \text{ mm}$

Length of tie Bar, L (Eq. 2.32) $= 686$

Increase length by 100 mm for loss of bond due to painting and another 50 mm for tolerance in placement $= 840 \text{ mm}$

Similarly, design thicknesses of flexible and rigid pavements for CBR of 4%, 5%, 6%, 8%, and 10% with design traffic of 2msa, 5msa, 10msa, 30msa, 50msa, 100msa, 150msa have been worked out and the thickness of flexible and rigid pavements have been presented in Chapter 5.

4 RATE ANALYSIS AND COST ESTIMATION

4.1 RATES OF VARIOUS ITEMS

The cost estimate is based upon rate analysis of Standard Data Book of MoRTH. The rates of aggregates and labour are as per Haryana Government approved rates, and rates of machinery are based upon Standard Data Book. The analysis of rates for per unit cost for various items of design are given in the following sections in Tables 4.1 to 4.10.

4.1.1 Subgrade

Compacting original ground (without borrowing from outside) supporting sub-grade taking output of 600 cum.

Table 4.1 Analysis of Rates for Subgrade

Item	Unit	Quantity	Rate	Amount (Rs.)
a) Labour				
Mate	day	0.120	506.15	60.74
Mazdoor	day	3.000	439.38	1318.14
b) Machinery				
Tractor with ripper	hour	9.000	327.00	2943.00
Motor grader for grading	hour	6.000	2009.00	12054.00
Water tanker 6 KL	hour	4.000	20.00	80.00
Vibratory roller 8-10 tonne @	hour	7.500	1292.00	9690.00
c) Material				
Cost of water	KL	24.000	20.00	480.00
d) Overhead charges @ 0.1 on (a+b+c)				2662.59
e) Contractor's profit @ 0.1 on (a+b+c+d)				2928.85
Cost for 600 cum = a+b+c+d+e				32217.31
Rate per cum = (a+b+c+d+e)/600				53.70
			say	_**54.00**_

4.1.2 Granular Subbase (GSB)

Construction of granular sub-base by providing close graded material, mixing in a mechanical mix plant at OMC, carriage of mixed material to work site, spreading in uniform layers with motor grader on prepared surface and compacting with vibratory power roller to achieve the desired density, output is taken as 225 cum (450 tonne).

Table 4.2 Analysis of Rates for Granular Sub base (GSB)

Item	Unit	Quantity	Rate	Amount (Rs.)
a) Labour				
Mate	day	0.400	506.15	202.46
Mazdoor skilled	day	2.000	529.84	1059.68
Mazdoor	day	8.000	439.38	3515.04
b) Machinery				
Wet mix plant @ 75 tonne capacity per hour	hour	6.000	1010.00	6060.00
Electric generator 125 KVA	hour	6.000	585.00	3510.00
Water tanker 6 KL capacity 5 km lead with one tripper hour	hour	4.500	20.00	90.00
Front end loader 1 cum bucket capacity	hour	6.000	676.00	4056.00
Tipper 10 tonne	tonne.km	450 x L	2.00	18000.00
Add 10 per cent of cost of carriage to cover loading and unloading				1800.00
Motor Grader 110 HP	hour	6.000	2009.00	12054.00
Vibratory roller 8-10 t	hour	6.000	1292.0	7752.00
c) Material				
Close graded Granular sub-base Material as per table 400-1				
For Grading-I Material				
53 mm to 9.5 mm @ 50 per cent	cum	144.000	676.00	97344.00
9.5 mm to 2.36 mm @ 20 per cent	cum	57.000	696.00	39672.00
2.36 mm below @ 30 per cent	cum	86.400	616.00	53222.40

Cost of water	KL	27.000	20.00	540.00
Rate per cum for grading-I Material				
d) Overhead charges @ 0.1 on (a+b+c)				24887.76
e) Contractor's profit @ 0.1 on (a+b+c+d)				27376.53
Cost for 225 cum = a+b+c+d+e				301141.87
Rate per cum = (a+b+c+d+e)/225				1338.41
			say	*__1338.00__*

4.1.3 Granular Base (WMM)

Providing, laying, spreading and compacting graded stone aggregate to wet mix macadam specification including premixing the material with water at OMC in mechanical mix plant carriage of mixed material by tipper to site, laying in uniform layers with paver in sub- base / base course on well prepared surface and compacting with vibratory roller to achieve the desired density, Output is taken as 225 cum.

Table 4.3 Analysis of Rates for Granular Base (WMM)

Item	Unit	Quantity	Rate	Amount (Rs.)
a) Labour				
Mate	day	0.480	506.15	242.95
Mazdoor skilled	day	2.000	529.84	1059.68
Mazdoor	day	10.000	439.38	4393.80
b) Machinery				
Wet mix plant of 75 tonne hourly capacity	hour	6.600	1010.00	6666.00
Electric generator 125 KVA	hour	6.000	585.00	3510.00
Front end loader 1 cum capacity	hour	6.000	676.00	4056.00
Paver finisher	hour	6.000	818.00	4908.00
Vibratory roller 8 - 10 tonne	hour	6x0.65	1292.00	5038.80
Or				
Smooth 3 wheeled	hour	12.000		

steel roller @ 8-10 tonnes.				
Water tanker 6 KL capacity	hour	3.000	20.00	60.00
Tipper	tonne.km	495 x L	2.00	19800.00
Add 10 per cent of cost of carriage to cover cost of loading and unloading				1980.00
c) Material				
45 mm to 22.4 mm@ 30 per cent	cum	89.100	723.00	64419.30
22.4 mm to 2.36 mm @ 40 per cent	cum	118.800	794.46	94381.37
2.36 mm to 75 micron@ 30 per cent	cum	89.100	239.00	21294.90
Cost of water	KL	18.000	20.00	360.00
d) Overhead charges @ 0.1 on (a+b+c)				23217.08
e) Contractor's profit @ 0.1 on (a+b+c+d)				25538.79
Cost for 225 cum = a+b+c+d+e				280926.67
Rate per cum = (a+b+c+d+e)/225				1248.56
			Say	***1249.00***

4.1.4 Prime Coat (PC)

Providing and applying primer coat with bitumen emulsion on prepared surface of granular base including clearing of road surface and spraying primer at the rate of 0.60 kg/sqm using mechanical means, Output taken is 3500 sqm.

Table 4.4 Analysis of Rates for Prime Coat

Item	Unit	Quantity	Rate	Amount (Rs.)
a) Labour				
Mate	day	0.080	506.15	40.49
Mazdoor	day	2.000	439.38	878.76

b) Machinery				
Mechanical broom @ 1250 sqm per hour	hour	2.800	299.00	837.20
Air compressor 250 cfm	hour	2.800	268.00	750.40
Bitumen pressure distributor @ 1750 sqm per hour	hour	2.000	900.00	1800.00
Water tanker 6 KL capacity @ 1 tripper hour	hour	1.000	20.00	20.00
c) Material				
Bitumen emulsion @ 0.6 kg per sqm	tonne	2.100	26840.00	56364.00
Cost of water	KL	6.000	20.00	120.00
d) Overhead charges @ 0.1 on (a+b+c)				6081.09
e) Contractor's profit @ 0.1 on (a+b+c+d)				6689.19
Cost for 3500 sqm = a+b+c+d+e				73581.13
Rate per cum = (a+b+c+d+e)/3500				21.02
			say	_**21.00**_

4.1.5 Tack Coat

Providing and applying tack coat with bitumen emulsion using emulsion pressure distributor at the rate of 0.20 kg per sqm on the prepared bituminous/granular surface cleaned with mechanical broom, Output taken as 3500 sqm.

Table 4.5 Analysis of Rates for Tack Coat

Item	Unit	Quantity	Rate	Amount (Rs.)
a) Labour				
Mate	day	0.080	506.15	40.49
Mazdoor	day	2.000	439.38	878.76
b) Machinery				
Mechanical broom @ 1250 sqm per hour	hour	2.800	299.00	837.20
Air compressor 250	hour	2.800	268.00	750.40

cfm				
Emulsion pressure distributor @ 1750 sqm per hour	hour	2.000	735.48	1470.96
c) Material				
Bitumen emulsion @ 0.2 kg per sqm	tonne	0.700	26840.00	18788.00
d) Overhead charges @ 0.1 on (a+b+c)				2276.58
e) Contractor's profit @ 0.1 on (a+b+c+d)				2504.24
Cost for 3500 sqm =				27546.63
Rate per cum =				7.87
			say	***8.00***

4.1.6 Dense Graded Bituminous Macadam (DBM)

Providing and laying dense graded bituminous macadam with 100-120 TPH batch type HMP producing an average output of 75 tonnes per hour using crushed aggregates of specified grading, premixed with bituminous binder @ 4.0 to 4.5 per cent by weight of total mix and filler, transporting the hot mix to work site, laying with a hydrostatic paver finisher with sensor control to the required grade, level and alignment, rolling with smooth wheeled, vibratory and tandem rollers to achieve the desired compaction as per MoRTH specification clause No. 507 complete in all respects, Output taken as 195 cum.

Table 4.6 Analysis of Rates for DBM

Item	Unit	Quantity	Rate	Amount (Rs.)
a) Labour				
Mate	day	0.840	506.15	425.17
Mazdoor working with HMP, mechanical broom, paver, roller, asphalt cutter and assistance for setting out lines, levels and layout of construction	day	16.000	439.38	7030.08

Skilled mazdoor for checking line & levels	day	5.000	529.84	2649.20
b) Machinery				
Batch mix HMP @ 75 tonne per hour	hour	6.000	14517.00	87102.00
Paver finisher hydrostatic with sensor control @ 75 cum per hour	hour	6.000	2243.00	13458.00
Generator 250 KVA	hour	6.000	585.00	3510.00
Front end loader 1 cum bucket capacity	hour	6.000	676.00	4056.00
Tipper 10 tonne capacity	tonne.km	450 x L	2.00	18000.00
Add 10 per cent of cost of carriage to cover cost of loading and unloading				1800.00
smooth wheeled roller 8-10 tonnes for initial break down rolling.	hour	6.00x0.65*	386.00	1505.40
Vibratory roller 8 tonnes for intermediate rolling.	hour	6.00x0.65*	1292.00	5038.80
Finish rolling with 6-8 tonnes smooth wheeled tandem roller.	hour	6.00x0.65*	959.00	3740.10
c) Materials				
Bitumen @ 4.25 per cent of weight of mix	tonne	19.130	31079.00	594541.27
Aggregate				
Total weight of mix = 450 tonnes				

Weight of bitumen = 19.13 tonnes				
Weight of aggregate = 450 - 19.13 = 430.87 tonnes				
Taking density of aggregate = 1.5 ton/cum				
Volume of aggregate = 287.25 cum				
Grading - I 40 mm (Nominal Size)				
37.5 - 25 mm 22 per cent	cum	63.190	676.00	42716.44
25 - 10 mm 13 per cent	cum	37.340	696.00	25988.64
10 -4.75 mm 19 per cent	cum	54.580	696.00	37987.68
4.75 mm and below 44 per cent	cum	126.390	616.00	77856.24
Filler @ 2 per cent of weight of aggregates.	tonne	8.620	523.00	4508.26
For Grading I (40 mm nominal size)				
d) **Overhead charges @ 0.1 on (a+b+c)**				93191.33
e) **Contractor's profit @ 0.1 on (a+b+c+d)**				102510.46
Cost for 195 cum = a+b+c+d+e				1127615.06
Rate per cum = (a+b+c+d+e)/195 (For Grading I)				5782.64
			say	***5783.00***

4.1.7 Semi-Dense Bituminous Concrete (SDBC)

Providing and laying semi dense bituminous concrete with 100-120 TPH batch type HMP producing an average output of 75 tonnes per hour using crushed aggregates of specified grading, premixed with bituminous binder @ 4.5 to 5 per cent of mix and filler, transporting the hot mix to work site, laying with a hydrostatic paver finisher with sensor control to the required grade, level and alignment, rolling with smooth wheeled, vibratory and tandem rollers to achieve the desired compaction as per MoRTH specification clause No. 508 complete in all respects, Output taken as 195 cum.

Table 4.7 Analysis of Rates for SDBC

Item	Unit	Quantity	Rate	Amount (Rs.)
a) Labour				
Mate	day	0.840	506.15	425.17
Mazdoor working with HMP, mechanical broom, paver, roller, asphalt cutter and assistance for setting out lines, levels and layout of construction	day	16.000	439.38	7030.08
Skilled mazdoor for checking line & levels	day	5.000	529.84	2649.20
b) Machinery				
Batch mix HMP @ 75 tonne per hour	hour	6.000	14517.00	87102.00
Paver finisher hydrostatic with sensor control @ 75 cum per hour	hour	6.000	2243.00	13458.00
Generator 250 KVA	hour	6.000	585.00	3510.00
Front end loader 1 cum bucket capacity	hour	6.000	676.00	4056.00
Tipper 10 tonne capacity	Tonne-km	450 x L	2.00	18000.00
Add 10 per cent of cost of carriage to cover cost of loading and unloading				1800.00

Smooth wheeled roller 8-10 tonnes for initial break down rolling.	hour	6.00x0.65*	386.00	1505.40
Vibratory roller 8 tonnes for intermediate rolling.	hour	6.00x0.65*	1292.00	5038.80
Finish rolling with 6-8 tonnes smooth wheeled tandem roller	hour	6.00x0.65*	959.00	3740.10
c) Material				
*** Grading I: 13 mm (Nominal Size)**				
i) Bitumen@ 4.5 per cent of weight of mix	tonne	20.250	31079.00	629349.75
ii) Aggregate				
Total weight of mix = 450 tonnes				
Weight of bitumen = 20.25 tonnes				
Weight of aggregate = 450-20.25 = 429.75 tonnes				
Taking density of aggregate = 1.5 ton/cum				
Volume of aggregate = 286.5 cum				
13.2 - 10 mm 20 per cent	cum	57.300	696.00	39880.80
10 - 5 mm 38 per cent	cum	108.870	696.00	75773.52
5 mm and below 40 per cent	cum	114.600	616.00	70593.60
Filler @ 2 per cent of weight of aggregates.	tonne	8.620	523.00	4508.26
for Grading I (13 mm nominal size)				
d) Overhead charges @ 0.1 on (a+b+c)				96842.07
e) Contractor's profit @ 0.1 on (a+b+c+d)				106526.27
Cost for 195 cum = a+b+c+d+e				1171789.02
Rate per cum = ((a+b+c+d+e)/195 (For Grading I)				6009.17
			Say	***6009.00***

4.1.8 Bituminous Concrete (BC)

Providing and laying bituminous concrete with 100-120 TPH batch type hot mix plant producing an average output of 75 tonnes per hour using crushed aggregates of specified grading, premixed with bituminous binder @ 5.4 to 5.6 per cent of mix and filler, transporting the hot mix to work site, laying with a hydrostatic paver finisher with sensor control to the required grade, level and alignment, rolling with smooth wheeled, vibratory and tandem rollers to achieve the desired compaction as per MORTH specification clause No. 509 complete in all respects, Output taken as 191 cum.

Table 4.8 Analysis of Rates for BC

Item	Unit	Quantity	Rate	Amount (Rs.)
a) Labour				
Mate	day	0.840	506.15	425.17
Mazdoor working with HMP, mechanical broom, paver, roller, asphalt cutter and assistance for setting out lines, levels and layout of construction	day	16.000	439.38	7030.08
Skilled mazdoor for checking line & levels	day	5.000	529.84	2649.20
b) Machinery				
Batch mix HMP @ 75 tonne per hour	hour	6.000	14517.00	87102.00
Paver finisher hydrostatic with sensor control @ 75 cum per hour	hour	6.000	2243.00	13458.00
Generator 250 KVA	hour	6.000	585.00	3510.00
Front end loader 1 cum bucket capacity	hour	6.000	676.00	4056.00
Tipper 10 tonne capacity	Tonne-km	450 x L	2.00	18000.00
Add 10 per cent of cost of carriage to cover cost of loading and unloading				1800.00
Smooth wheeled roller 8-10 tonnes for initial break down	hour	6.00x0.65*	386.00	1505.40

rolling.				
Vibratory roller 8 tonnes for intermediate rolling.	hour	6.00x0.65*	1292.00	5038.80
Finish rolling with 6-8 tonnes smooth wheeled tandem roller.	hour	6.00x0.65*	959.00	3740.10
c) Material				
i) Bitumen@ 5 per cent of weight of mix	tonne	22.500	31079.00	699277.50
ii) Aggregate				
Total weight of mix = 450 tonnes				
Weight of bitumen = 22.5 tonnes				
Weight of aggregate = 450 - 22.50 = 427.50 tonnes				
Taking density of aggregate = 1.5 ton/cum				
Volume of aggregate = 285 cum				
Grading - II-13 mm (Nominal Size)				
13.2 - 10 mm30 per cent	cum	85.500	696.00	59508.00
10 - 5 mm 25 per cent	cum	71.250	696.00	49590.00
5 mm and below43 per cent	cum	122.550	616.00	75490.80
Filler @ 2 per cent of weight of aggregates.	tonne	8.620	523.00	4508.26
For Grading-II (10 mm nominal size)				
d) Overhead charges @ 0.1 on (a+b+c)				103668.93
e) Contractor's profit @ 0.1 on (a+b+c+d)				114035.82
Cost for 191 cum = a+b+c+d+e				1254394.0
Rate per cum = (a+b+c+d+e)/191 (For Grading-II)				6567.51
			say	***6568.00***

4.1.9 Dry Lean Cement Concrete Sub-base (DLC)

Construction of dry lean cement concrete Sub- base over a prepared sub-grade with coarse and fine aggregate conforming to IS: 383, the size of coarse aggregate not exceeding 25 mm, aggregate cement ratio not to exceed 15:1, aggregate gradation after blending to be as per table 600-1, cement content not to be less than 150 kg/ cum, optimum moisture content to be determined during trial length construction, concrete strength not to be less than 10 Mpa at 7 days, mixed in a batching plant, transported to site, laid with a paver with electronic sensor, compacting with 8-10 tonnes vibratory roller, finishing and curing. Output taken as 450 cum.

Table 4.9 Analysis of Rates for DLC Subbase

Item	Unit	Quantity	Rate	Amount (Rs.)
a) Labour				
Mate	day	1.120	506.15	566.89
Mazdoor skilled	day	6.000	529.84	3179.04
Mazdoor	day	22.000	439.38	9666.36
b) Machinery				
Front end loader 1 cum bucket capacity	hour	6.000	676.00	4056.00
Cement concrete batch mix plant @ 75 cum per hour	hour	6.000	5304.00	31824.00
Electric generator 100 KVA	hour	6.000	585.00	3510.00
Paver with electronic sensor	hour	6.000	2243.00	13458.00
Vibratory roller 8-10 t capacity	hour	8.000	1292.00	10336.00
Water tanker6 KL capacity	hour	8.000	20.00	160.00
Tipper	tonne.km	990 x L	2.00	39600.00
Add 10 per cent of cost of carriage to cover cost of loading and unloading				3960.00
c) Material				
Crushed stone coarse aggregate of 25 mm and 12.5 mm nominal sizes graded as per table 600-1 @ 0.90 cum/cum of concrete conforming to clause 602.2.4.	cum	405.000	1008.00	408240.00

Coarse Sand as per IS: 383 @ 0.45 cum/cum of concrete	cum	203.000	385.00	78155.00
Cement @ 150 kg/cum of concrete	tonne	67.500	6000.00	405000.00
Cost of water	KL	48.000	20.00	960.00
d) Overhead charges @ 0.1 on (a+b+c)				101267.13
e) Contractor's profit @ 0.1 on (a+b+c+d)				111393.84
Cost for 450 cum = a+b+c+d+e				1225332.26
Rate per cum = (a+b+c+d+e)/450				2722.96
			say	___2723.00___

4.1.10 Pavement Quality Concrete (PQC)

Construction of un-reinforced, dowel jointed, plain cement concrete pavement over a prepared sub base with 43 grade cement @ 400 kg per cum, coarse and fine aggregate conforming to IS 383, maximum size of coarse aggregate not exceeding 25 mm, mixed in a batching and mixing plant as per approved mix design, transported to site, laid with a fixed form or slip form paver, spread, compacted and finished in a continuous operation including provision of contraction, expansion, construction and longitudinal joints, joint filler, separation membrane, sealant primer, joint sealant, debonding strip, dowel bar, tie rod, admixtures as approved, curing compound, finishing to lines and grades as per drawing, Output taken as 1050 cum.

Table 4.10 Analysis of Rates for PQC

Item	Unit	Quantity	Rate	Amount (Rs.)
a) Labour				
Mate	day	2.000	506.15	1012.30
Mazdoor skilled	day	15.000	529.84	7947.60
Mazdoor	day	35.000	439.38	15378.30
b) Machinery				
Road Sweeper @ 1250 sqm per hour	hour	2.800	299.00	837.20
Front end loader 1 cum bucket capacity	hour	18.000	676.00	12168.00

Cement concrete batch mix plant @ 175 cum per hour (effective output)	hour	6.000	10920.00	65520.00
Electric generator 250 KVA	hour	6.000	585.00	3510.00
Slip form paver with electronic sensor	hour	6.000	2405.00	14430.00
Water tanker6 KL capacity	hour	36.000	20.00	720.00
Transit truck agitator 5 cum capacity.	tonne.km	2415xL	4.32	208656.00
Add 10 per cent of cost of carriage to cover cost of loading and unloading				20865.60
Concrete joint cutting machine.	hour	12.000	105.00	1260.00
Texturing machine.	hour	12.000	128.00	1536.00
c) Material				
Crushed stone coarse aggregates of 25mm and 12.5mm nominal size @ 0.90 cum/cum of concrete conforming to clause 602.2.4..	cum	945.000	1008.00	952560.00
Sand as per IS: 383 and conforming to clause 602.2.4 @ 0.45 cum/cum of concrete	cum	473.000	385.00	182105.00
Cement 43 grade @ 400 kg/cum of concrete	tonne	414.000	6000.00	2484000.00
32 mm mild steel dowel bars of grade S 240	tonne	9.450	48000.00	453600.00
16 mm deformed steel tie bars of grade S 415	tonne	1.170	50800.00	59436.00
Separation Membrane of impermeable plastic sheeting 125 micron thick	sqm	3675.000	38.00	139650.00
Pre moulded Joint filler, 25 mm thick for expansion joint.	sqm	16.330	708.07	11562.79
Joint sealant	kg	875.000	145.00	126875.00
Sealant primer	kg	116.670	490.00	57168.30
Plastic sheath,1.25 mm thick for dowel bars	sqm	46.670	48.00	2240.16
Curing compound	liter	1850.000	93.00	172050.00

Super plasticizer admixture IS marked as per 9103-1999 @ 0.5 per cent by weight of cement	Kg	2070.000	50.00	103500.00
Cost of water	KL	216.000	20.00	4320.00
Add 1 per cent of material for cost of miscellaneous materials like tarpauline, Hessian cloth, metal cap, cotton / compressible sponge and cradle for dowel bars, work bridges for men to approach concrete surface without walking over it, cutting blades and bites, minor equipments like scrabbling machine, threads, ropes, guide wires and any other unforeseen items.				47490.67
d) Overhead charges @ 0.1 on (a+b+c)				515039
e) Contractor's profit @ 0.1 on (a+b+c+d)				566543
Cost for 1050cum = a+b+c+d+e				6231982
Rate per cum = (a+b+c+d+e)/1050				***5935.00***

4.2 COST ESTIMATION

Construction Cost of Flexible and Rigid Pavements has been estimated using Standard Data Book of MoRTH (2003). The maintenance cost of pavements has been calculated with previous experience.

4.2.1 Cost Estimation of a flexible pavement section of 1 km length for 4% CBR and 2 msa design traffic

Maintenance Cost for Flexible Pavement of 1km length for 15 years life period has been calculated as;

For initial 4 years of life period the maintenance Cost   = 0.7 lakh per year
$$= 0.7*4   = 2.8 \text{ lakh}$$
For 5th year a layer has been provided with (SDBC+TC)
Cost = 9.013+0.675   = 9.688 lakh
For 6-9 years life period the maintenance cost = 0.7*4 = 2.8 lakh

For 10th year a layer has been provide with (SDBC+TC)

Cost = 9.013+0.675 = 9.688 lakh

For 11-15 years period the maintenance cost = 0.7*5 = 3.5 lakh

Maintenance Cost for life period of 15 years

= 2.8+9.688+2.8+9.688+3.5 = 28.327 lakh

Say = 28 Lakhs

Table 4.11 Cost estimation of a Flexible pavement section of 1km length for 4% CBR and 2 msa design traffic

S No	Item	Dimensions			Unit	Quan-tity	Rate per unit Lakh#	Total Cost Lakh#	Main-ten-ance Cost Lakh
		Leng-th (m)	Width (m)	Thick-ness (m)					
		1	2	3	4	5 =1*2*3	6	7 =(5*6)	8
A	Subgrade	1000	7.5	0.500	Cum	3750	54	2.2125	
B	GSB	1000	7.5	0.265	Cum	1987.5	1472	29.256	
C	WMM	1000	7.5	0.225	Cum	1687.5	1373	23.169	
D	PC+TC	1000	7.5	0	Sqm	7500	32	2.4	
E	DBM	1000	7.5	0.050	Cum	375	5783	21.686	28
F	TC	1000	7.5	0	Sqm	7500	9	0.675	
G	SDBC	1000	7.5	0.020	Cum	150	6009	9.013	
Construction Cost per km (**Rs in Lakhs**)								83	
Total Cost (**Rs in Lakhs**)								111	

one lakh Rs. = 0.1 million rupees

4.2.2 Cost Estimation of a rigid pavement section of 1 km length for 4% CBR and 2 msa design traffic

Maintenance Cost for Rigid Pavement of 1km length for 15 years life period has been calculated as;

For 15 years life period the Maintenance Cost (**Lakhs**) = 0.2 per year

= 0.2*15 = 3.0 Lakh

Table 4.12 Cost estimation of a Rigid Pavement section of 1km length for 4% CBR and 2msa traffic value

S. No.	Item	Dimensions			Unit	Quan -tity	Rate per Unit	Cost	Main -ten -ance Cost
		Leng -th (m)	Width (m)	Thick -ness (m)		(m³)		Lakh	Lakh
		1	2	3	4	5 =1*2*3	6	7 =5*6	8
A	Subgrade	1000	7.5	0.5	Cum	3750	59	2.2125	
B	GSB	1000	7.5	0.15	Cum	1125	1472	16.560	
C	DLC	1000	7.5	0.15	Cum	1125	2723	30.6337	3
D	PQC	1000	7.5	0.23	Cum	1725	6529	112.6252	
Construction Cost per km (**Rs in Lakhs**)								150	
Total Cost per km (**Rs in Lakhs**)								153	

As given in Table 4.11 and Table 4.12, the Cost Estimation has been done on the same line for flexible and rigid pavement sections of 1km length for other values of CBR also such as 4%, 5%, 6%, 8%, 10% and design traffic of 2msa, 5msa, 10msa, 20msa, 30msa, 50msa, 100msa and 150msa and then total cost of each pavement section has been estimated presented in Chapter 6.

5 THICKNESS AND COST VARIATION

5.1 VARIATION IN PAVEMENT THICKNESS WITH SUBGRADE STRENGTH AND DESIGN TRAFFIC

A 7.5 m carriageway road has been designed both for flexible and rigid pavement for given values of design traffic of 2msa, 5msa, 10msa, 20msa, 30msa, 50msa, 100msa and 150msa and Subgrade effective CBR of 4%, 5%, 6%, 8% and 10% as per guidelines of IRC:37-2012 and IRC 58:2015 respectively. Details of axle load spectrum of rear single, tandem and tridem axles are taken from IRC 58:2015. The design thicknesses are worked out for varying values of design traffic and effective CBR of subgrade following the same method as given in the previous chapter. The thicknesses so obtained are given in table 5.1 and table 5.2 respectively.

5.1.1 Variation in Flexible Pavement thickness with CBR and Design Traffic

Table 6.1. Thickness of Flexible Pavement in mm for various values of CBR of subgrade and design traffic

Soil	Design Traffic (msa)							
CBR (%)	2	5	10	20	30	50	100	150
4	560	620	700	730	750	750	770	785
5	510	580	660	690	710	715	730	745
6	470	535	655	640	655	660	685	700
8	445	475	550	575	590	590	615	635
10	445	475	550	570	585	585	610	625

Fig. 5.1 shows the variation in thickness of Flexible Pavement with different values of subgrade strength and design traffic. It is observed that the thickness increases with increase in traffic and it decreases with increase in subgrade CBR. It is also observed that total thickness of flexible pavement decreases with increase in CBR value only up to 8% CBR of Subgrade and there is no significant dcrease in the thickness of flexible pavement from 8% to 10% CBR for all values of design traffic from 2msa, to 150msa.

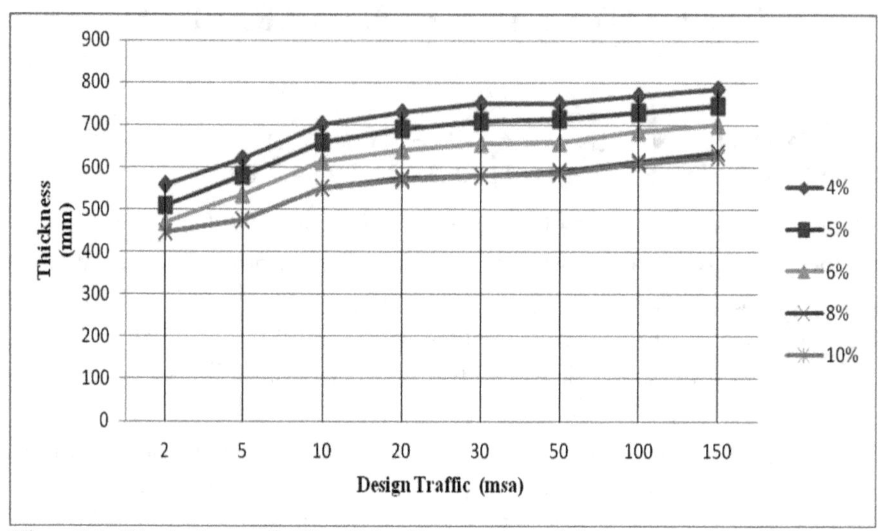

Fig. 5.1 Variation of Flexible Pavement thickness with CBR and Design Traffic

5.1.2 Variation of Rigid Pavement thickness with CBR and Design Traffic value

Table 5.2. Thickness of Rigid Pavement in mm for various values of CBR of subgrade and equivalent design traffic

Soil CBR (%)	*Equivalent Design Traffic (msa) at the end of design life							
	2	5	10	20	30	50	100	150
4	230	240	250	260	260	270	280	280
5	230	240	250	260	260	270	280	270
6	230	240	250	260	260	270	280	280
8	230	240	250	260	260	270	280	280
10	230	240	250	260	260	270	280	280

* Equivalent design traffic is traffic in msa of CVs in both directions at the end of design life with same initial number of CVs as that for flexible pavement design. This traffic is further multiplied with LDF of 0.25 to get total design traffic which is further split into 6-hr day time and 6-hr night time design msa for fatigue analysis of BUC and TDC respectively.

Fig. 5.2 shows the variation in thickness of Rigid Pavement with different values of subgrade strength and design traffic.

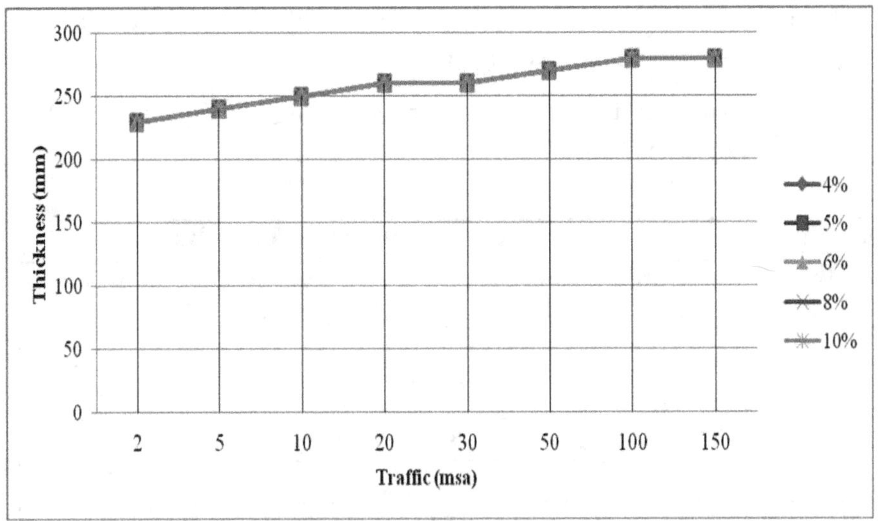

Fig. 5.2 Thickness variation of Rigid Pavement with Soil CBR and Equivalent Traffic Value

It is observed from Fig. 6.2 that there is no significant variation in the thickness of rigid pavement for improvement in subgrade strength from 4% to 10% CBR. However, increase in design traffic causes an increase in thickness of the pavement.

5.2 VARIATION IN COST OF PAVEMENTS WITH SUBGRADE CBR AND DESIGN TRAFFIC

5.2.1 Variation in Cost of Flexible and Rigid Pavement for Subgrade CBR 4% with Design Traffic

The cost of flexible and rigid pavements for subgrade CBR value of 4.0% for various values of design traffic from 2 msa to 150 msa for a design period of 15 years design life is given in Table 5.3 for 1 km length of the pavement. It is observed that initial cost of construction increases for both the pavements with increase in design traffic. The maintenance cost of flexible pavement also increases with design traffic whereas maintenance cost of rigid pavement remains the same with increase in design traffic. The initial cost of construction of a rigid pavement is more than the initial cost of construction of a flexible pavement for the same design traffic. However, this difference in cost of construction reduces for higher values of design traffic. It is also observed from Table 5.3 and Figure 5.3 that total cost of construction and maintenance over the design life is more for rigid pavement only up to a design traffic of 5msa after which the total cost is less for rigid pavements by about 2% to 18% of the total cost of flexible pavement depending upon the design traffic.

Table 5.3 Variation in total cost for 1km length of pavement for Subgrade CBR 4%

Design Traffic (msa)	Cost of Pavements per km in Lakh Rs.					
	Flexible Pavement			Rigid Pavement		
	Construc -tion Cost	Mainte -nance Cost	Total Cost	Construc -tion Cost	Mainte -nance Cost	Total Cost
2	83	28	111	150 (81)	3	153 (38)
5	94	33	127	155 (65)		158 (24)
10	116	50	165	159 (34)		162 (-2)
20	129	50	178	163 (23)		166 (-7)
30	137	50	187	163 (19)		166 (-11)
50	137	50	187	168 (19)		171 (-9)
100	147	60	213	172 (14)		175 (-18)
150	153	60	213	172 (10)		175 (-18)

( ) indicates percentage increase in construction cost and total cost of rigid pavement over flexible pavement cost.

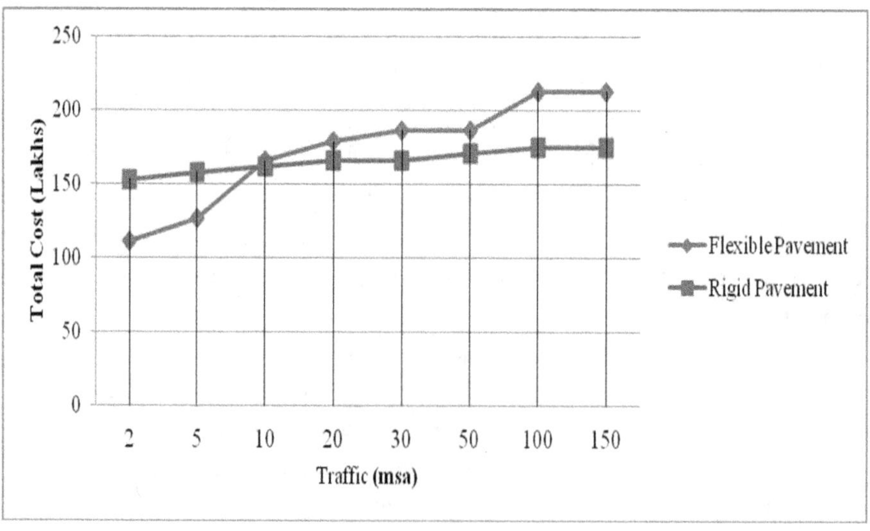

Fig. 5.3 Variation of Total Cost for Subgrade CBR of 4% for Flexible and Rigid Pavement

5.2.2 Variation in Cost of Flexible and Rigid Pavements for Subgrade CBR 5% with design Traffic

Table 5.4 Variation in total cost for 1km length of pavement for subgrade CBR 5%

Design Traffic (msa)	Cost of Pavements per km in Lakh Rs.					
	Flexible Pavement			Rigid Pavement		
	Construc-tion Cost	Mainte-nance Cost	Total Cost	Construc-tion Cost	Mainte-nance Cost	Total Cost
2	78	28	106	150 (92)	3	153 (44)
5	88	33	121	155 (76)		158 (31)
10	108	50	158	159 (44)		162 (3)
20	121	50	171	163 (31)		166 (-3)
30	130	50	180	163 (25)		166 (-8)
50	132	50	182	168 (23)		171 (-6)
100	139	60	199	172 (21)		175 (-12)
150	145	60	205	172 (15)		175 (-15)

( ) indicates percentage increase in construction cost of rigid pavement over flexible pavement cost.

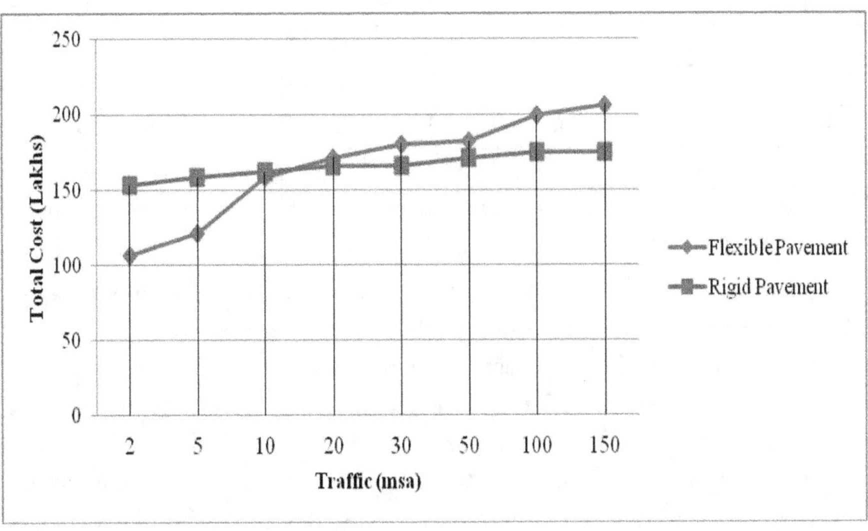

Fig. 5.4 Variation of Total Cost for Subgrade CBR of 5% for Flexible and Rigid Pavement

It is observed from Table 5.4 and Figure 5.4 that the cost of construction of rigid pavement is more by 15 to 92% for various values of design traffic from 150 msa to 2 msa. However, as seen from Fig. 5.4, the total cost of Rigid Pavement is more than the total cost of Flexible pavement only up to 10 msa design traffic and for higher values of design traffic, the cost of Flexible Pavement is higher than the cost of Rigid Pavement by 3% to 15%.

5.2.3 Variation in Cost of Flexible and Rigid Pavements for Subgrade CBR 6% with Design Traffic

Table 5.5 Variation in total cost for 1km length of pavement for Subgrade CBR 6%

| Design Traffic (msa) | Cost of Pavements per km in Lakhs Rs. | | | | | |
| | Flexible Pavement | | | Rigid Pavement | | |
	Construc -tion Cost	Mainte -nance Cost	Total Cost	Construc -tion Cost	Mainte -nance Cost	Total Cost
2	74	28	102	150 (103)	3	153 (50)
5	82	33	115	155 (89)		158 (37)
10	102	50	152	159 (56)		162 (7)
20	113	50	163	163 (44)		166 (2)
30	120	50	170	163 (36)		166 (-2)
50	121	50	171	168 (38)		171 (-1)
100	133	60	193	172 (29)		175 (-9)
150	139	60	199	172 (23)		175 (-13)

( ) indicates percentage increase in construction cost of rigid pavement over flexible pavement cost.

Variation in cost of Flexible and Rigid Pavements for Subgrade CBR of 6% with various values of design traffic has been shown in Fig. 5.5. It is observed from Table 5.5 and Figure 5.5 that the cost of construction of rigid pavement is more by 23 to 103% for various values of design traffic from 150 msa to 2 msa. However, as seen from Fig. 5.5, the total cost of Rigid Pavement is more than the total cost of Flexible pavement only up to 20 msa design traffic and for higher values of design traffic, the cost of Flexible Pavement becomes higher than the cost of Rigid Pavement by 2% to 13%.

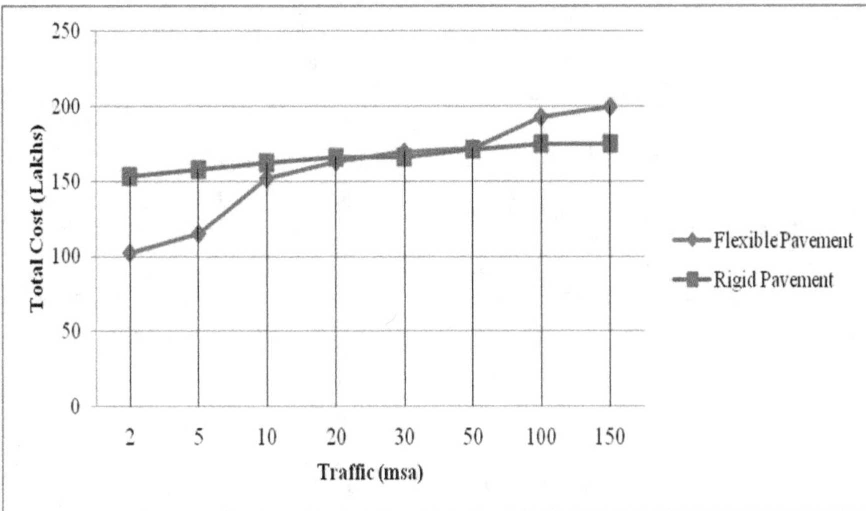

Fig. 5.5 Variation of Total Cost for Subgrade CBR of 6% for Flexible and Rigid Pavement

5.2.4 Variation in Cost of Flexible and Rigid Pavements for Subgrade CBR 8% with Design Traffic

Table 5.6 Variation in total cost for 1km length of pavement for Subgrade CBR 8%

Design Traffic (msa)	Cost of Pavements per km in Lakhs Rs.					
	Flexible Pavement			Rigid Pavement		
	Construc-tion Cost	Mainte-nance Cost	Total Cost	Construc-tion Cost	Mainte-nance Cost	Total Cost
2	72	28	100	150 (108)	3	153 (53)
5	76	33	109	155 (104)		158 (45)
10	94	50	144	159 (69)		162 (13)
20	105	50	155	163 (55)		166 (7)
30	107	50	157	163 (52)		166 (6)
50	111	50	161	168 (51)		171 (6)
100	123	60	180	172 (40)		175 (-3)
150	131	60	191	172 (31)		175 (-8)

( ) indicates percentage increase in construction cost of rigid pavement over flexible pavement cost.

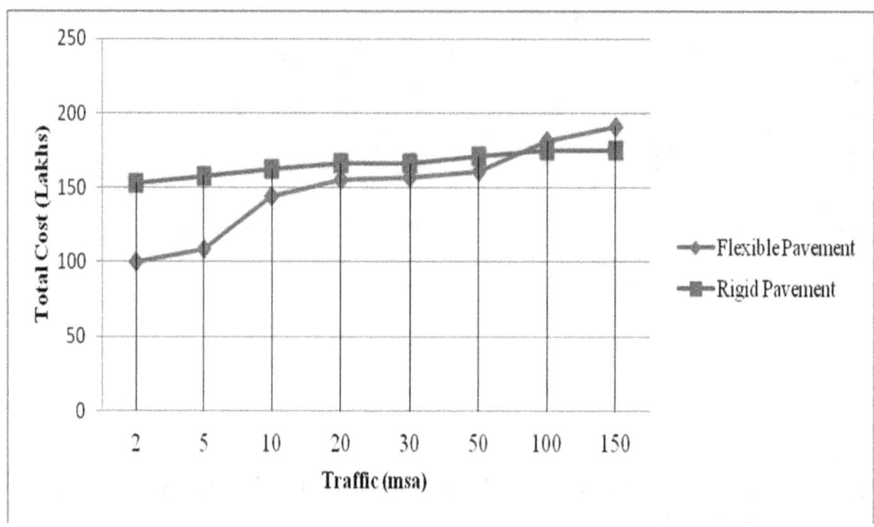

Fig. 5.6 Variation of Total Cost for Subgrade CBR of 8% for Flexible and Rigid Pavement

It is observed from Table 5.6 and Figure 5.6 that the cost of construction of rigid pavement is more by 31 to 108% for various values of design traffic from 150 msa to 2 msa. However, as seen from Fig. 5.6, the total cost of Rigid Pavement is more than the total cost of Flexible pavement only up to 50msa design traffic and for higher values of design traffic, the cost of Flexible Pavement becomes higher than the cost of Rigid Pavement by 3% to 8%.

5.2.5 Variation in Cost of Flexible and Rigid Pavements for Subgrade CBR 10% with Design Traffic

It is observed from Table 5.7 that the cost of construction of rigid pavement is more by 35% to 108% for various values of design traffic from 150 msa to 2 msa. However, as seen from Figure 5.7, the total cost of Rigid Pavement is more than the total cost of Flexible pavement up to 50msa design traffic and then for remaining values of design traffic only up to 150 msa design traffic and for higher values of design traffic the cost of Flexible Pavement becomes higher than the cost of Rigid Pavement by 3% to 6%.

Table 5.7 Variation in total cost for 1km length of pavement for Subgrade CBR 10%

Design Traffic (msa)	Cost of Pavements per km in Lakhs Rs.					
	Flexible Pavement			Rigid Pavement		
	Construc-tion Cost	Mainte-nance Cost	Total Cost	Construc-tion Cost	Mainte-nance Cost	Total Cost
2	72	28	100	150 (108)	3	153 (53)
5	76	33	109	155 (104)		158 (45)
10	94	50	144	159 (69)		162 (13)
20	102	50	152	163 (58)		166 (8)
30	107	50	157	163 (52)		166 (6)
50	109	50	159	168 (54)		171 (8)
100	120	60	180	172 (42)		175 (-3)
150	127	60	187	172 (35)		175 (-6)

() indicates percentage increase in construction cost of rigid pavement over flexible pavement cost.

Variation in Cost of Flexible and Rigid Pavements for Subgrade CBR 10% with various design traffic has been shown in Fig. 5.7

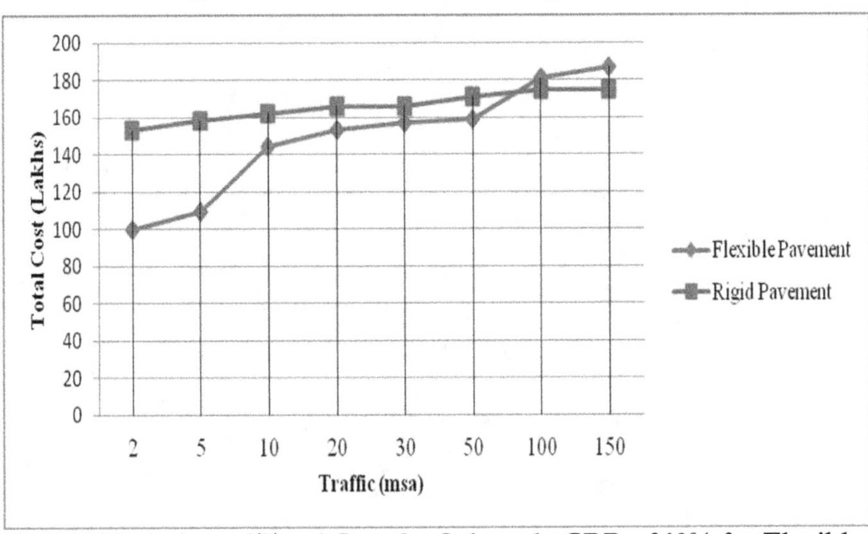

Fig. 5.7 Variation of Total Cost for Subgrade CBR of 10% for Flexible and Rigid Pavement

S.N. Sachdeva

72

6 ECONOMY OF DESIGN

6.1 GENERAL

Flexible and Rigid pavements are the two main type of road pavements that are used the world over. Flexible pavements are the bituminous pavements and rigid pavements are the cement concrete pavements. In countries like India and other countries of the world as well, bituminous pavements are used on majority of the roads because of their low initial cost of construction, ease of construction and maintenance, and faster progress of construction work. However, the maintenance cost of bituminous pavements is quite high. The total cost of construction over the design life in case of concrete roads may be much less than bituminous roads. However, this concept is usually not clear to the professionals that for what values of subgrade strength and design traffic, a concrete pavement would be more economical. Designs and their cost estimation have been made in the preceding chapters for a 7.5 m carriageway road both for bituminous and concrete pavements for varying values of subgrade strength from CBR value of 4% to 10% and design traffic of 2 msa to 150 msa. The following sections further discuss the economy of these two type of pavements under these varying conditions.

6.2 EFFECT OF SUBGRADE STRENGTH AND TRAFFIC ON THICKNESS OF PAVEMENTS

(i) The thickness of Bituminous Pavement decreases by about 20% with increase in the value of CBR of subgrade from 4% to 10% for all values of design traffic from 2 msa to 150 msa.

(ii) There is no significant variation in the thickness of Rigid Pavement with increase in subgrade CBR from 4% to 10%.

(iii) The thickness of Bituminous Pavement increases by about 40% to 50% with increase in the value of design traffic from 2 msa to 150 msa for all values of subgrade strength from CBR 4% to 10%.

(iv) The thickness of Concrete Pavement increases by about 17% to 20% with increase in the value of design traffic from 2 msa to 150 msa for all values of subgrade strength from CBR 4% to 10%.

(v) A given increase in traffic causes more increase in the thickness of a bituminous pavement than a rigid pavement.

(vi) The Rigid Pavements can sustain more design traffic with a little increase in pavement thickness.

6.3 EFFECT OF SUBGRADE STRENGTH AND TRAFFIC ON COST OF PAVEMENTS

(i)   The cost of Flexible Pavement decreases with increase in the value of CBR from 4% to 10% for a given design traffic. However, the decrease in cost when CBR increases from 8% to 10% is only marginal.

(ii) There is no significant variation in the total cost of Rigid Pavement with increase in the value of CBR from 4% to 10% for a given design traffic.

(iii) Maintenance Cost of Flexible Pavements for entire design life is very high and may be 9 to 20 times costlier with design traffic varying from 2 msa to 150 msa as compared to the maintenance cost of Rigid Pavements.

(iv) Maintenance Cost for Flexible Pavements increases with increase in the design traffic but for Rigid Pavements there is little change in the Maintenance Cost.

(v)   A concrete pavement may prove to be more economical in its total cost when (a) CBR of subgrade is 4% and design traffic is 10 msa or higher, (b) CBR of subgrade is 5% and design traffic is 20 msa or higher, (c) CBR of subgrade is 6% and design traffic is 30 msa or higher, and (d) CBR of subgrade is 8% to 10% with design traffic of 100 msa or higher.

(vi) For low design traffic the flexible pavements are more economical than the rigid pavements for any value of CBR of subgrade. However, as design traffic becomes more, the Rigid Pavements are more economical than the Flexible Pavements due to increased cost of bituminous pavements at higher traffic levels and low maintenance cost of rigid pavements.

xxxxxxxxx

References

1. AASHTO 1993, AASHTO guide for design of pavement structures, American Association of State Highway and Transportation Officials, Washington D.C.

2. IRC:15-2011, Sstandard specifications and code of practice for construction of concrete roads, Indian Roads Congress, New Delhi.

3. IRC:37-2012, Guidelines for the Design of Flexible Pavements, Indian Roads Congress, New Delhi.

4. IRC-58:2015, Guidelines for design of plain jointed rigid pavements for highway, Indian Roads Congress, New Delhi.

5. IRC-SP:49-2014, Guidelines for the use of Dry lean concrete as sub-base for rigid pavement (first revision), Indian Road Congress, August 2014, New Delhi.

6. IS 456-2000, Plain and reinforced concrete-code of practice (fourth revision), Bureau of Indian Standards, New Delhi.

7. IS 9214-1974, Method of determination of modulus of subgrade reaction of soil in field, Bureau of Indian Standards, August 1997, New Delhi.

8. MoRTH (2003), Standard data book for analysis of rates, Ministry of Road Transport and Highways, Indian Roads Congress, New Delhi.

9. MoRTH (2013), Specifications for Road and Bridge Works, Ministry of Road Transport and Highways, Indian Roads Congress, New Delhi.